Mass Media Violence and Society

Mass Media Violence and Society

DENNIS HOWITT, B.Tech., D.Phil.,
Research Officer at the Centre for Mass
Communications Research, University of Leicester
and
GUY CUMBERBATCH, B.A., Ph.D.,
Lecturer in Applied Psychology, University
of Aston in Birmingham

A HALSTED PRESS BOOK

JOHN WILEY & SONS
New York

© Paul Elek (Scientific Books) Ltd. 1975
First Published in Great Britain in 1975
by Paul Elek (Scientific Books) Ltd.,
54-58 Caledonian Road, London N1 9RN

Published in the U.S.A.
by Halsted Press, a Division of
John Wiley & Sons, Inc.
New York

Howitt, Dennis.
    Mass media, violence and society

A Halsted Press book.
Includes indexes.

1. Violence in mass media.   2. Mass media-Social
aspects–United States.   I. Cumberbatch, Guy, joint author.
II. Title.

HN90.M3H68 1975   301.16'1   74-26193
ISBN 0-470-41745-5

CONTENTS

INTRODUCTION

The central theme of this book is that the Mass Media do not have any significant effect on the level of violence in society. This view arises from our consideration of the available social scientific research from social psychology, experimental psychology, sociology, and psychiatry. However, in arguing that the weight of the evidence is against any adverse effects of the media, we violate what would appear to be the established wisdom of social science and that of popular mythology. The public debate on media violence shows little sign of abating and, indeed, has received fresh impetus from the rapid growth since the early 1960s, of social scientific research into the problem. Millions of dollars have been spent by American commissions over the last few years — the Eisenhower commission into the causes and prevention of violence published in 1969 and the U.S. Surgeon General's study published in 1971. The conclusions to these massive financial investments were that there is some causal relationship between media violence and violence in real life. In this book we review this research and must demur from the conclusions which have been reached in the past. In many ways the task of reviewing the research would have been much easier if we had simply reiterated the conventional conclusions of researchers and concurred with the general belief that media violence is harmful. Had we done so, then it seems to us that this book would have made no sense whatsoever. In order to render a meaningful account of the relevant research it is not enough to simply show that there are a number of studies which acclaim the media's responsibility for causing violence. We must examine the individual worth of each study, question the meaning of each piece of research in its own terms and gauge the extent to which different studies are compatible with each other and imply similar policy decisions. Without this book there would be no argument commonly available to the layman to help him evaluate the somewhat ambiguous social science research. Social science would have duped him by giving easy answers to complex problems.

We would like to express our appreciation to all of those who have helped us in so many ways in the last few years. Special thanks are due to Richard Dembo and Roy Davies for encouragement and help in the preparation of this manuscript. Of course, the arguments and opinions we offer are not necessarily shared by any institution to which we may be affiliated.

CHAPTER ONE
THE PUBLIC DEBATE

'. . . What's the matter you dissentious rogues,
That, rubbing the poor itch of your opinion,
Make yourselves scabs?'

Coriolanus I (i) 171

Samuel Butler once said that the wish to spread those opinions which we hold conducive to our own welfare is so deeply rooted in the English character that few of us can escape its influence.[1] Perhaps there is nothing peculiarly English about this phenomenon but it certainly exists.

What is so intriguing about the notion of public opinion is that it is such a surprisingly ambiguous phenomenon. People spread rather different opinions in different contexts and different people spread their opinions in different ways. What this means is that any attempt to describe public opinion on an issue and infer a level of public concern can be misleading. Rather than speak of public opinion as if it could be measured simply and uniquely in the sort of way that temperature is measured using a thermometer, it is more accurate to say that there are a number of images of public opinion available some of which are much more amenable to measurement than others. In this chapter we shall examine three different images of public opinion on mass media violence. This chapter attempts, therefore, to describe the perceived public concern about violence in the mass media.

The first image of public opinion is that which emerges in the public debate which is part of our daily lives. This debate is conducted by a myriad of informal groups thrown up by accident or design of time and place: the home, the pub, the school, the launderette. Debate may be a little too grand a concept to describe what actually goes on when opinions are exchanged at this informal level, but it is none the less a public debate and it reflects public concern and public opinion. There are considerable problems in measuring this natural public opinion without distorting the true image. However, later in this chapter we shall consider some evidence regarding spontaneous opinion and everyday behaviour which is relevant to this image of the public's concern over mass media violence.

The second image of public opinion emerges from the social

1

scientist's attempt to measure this public opinion in a formal and objective way. He does this by public opinion polls and often achieves a fair degree of accuracy in such areas as voting behaviour. The logic of the method is that if a small number of people are selected quite randomly then the chances are that these are fairly representative of the larger population.[2] Unfortunately, what people say when interviewed may not be quite the same thing that they say to friends or it may even be something that they never thought about. Thus, we may have a situation where public opinion polls actually do measure a *public* opinion, whereas we may be more interested in the *private* opinion which is exchanged amid informal groups.

The distinction between these two measures of public opinion was hinted at by the Independent Television Authority in an article in *The Times* (28.8.70).

The public are far more disposed to accept the general proposition that violence on television is harmful when put to them than they are to react spontaneously against particular scenes of violence which they encounter in their viewing.

There is a further image of public opinion which is probably the most influential of all for decision making. This is the public opinion reported in the mass media itself. This image of public opinion is represented by the views of people who appear in the newspapers, on television and on the radio. Probably for most people the image of public debate is formed by the news of this debate rather than any objective, and little publicised, public opinion poll. In many ways it is surprising to note how much of the news in newspapers is in fact merely opinion made newsworthy by the context and the author of the statements. For instance, in an unpublished study of the ways in which the mass media report events in Northern Ireland, it was found that the largest category of news was that devoted to the speeches and comments of people (mainly politicians).[3] The importance of the mass media public debates stems mainly from the nature of those whose views are being expressed. These will tend to be authoritative and high credibility sources who can form important and powerful pressure groups on the policy making which affects the general public. For this reason the present chapter will later concentrate on the opinion which is expressed in the mass media debate. This debate is also more interesting from an analytic point of view in that the logic behind the opinion may be revealed.

It is very difficult to place the public debate on mass media violence in any general context. All that can be said is that public opinion polls have tended to show a large percentage of the population to be concerned in one way or another over the problem. The most recent of such polls by Opinion Research Centre (1973) in this country gave the following figures for people's views on television.[4]

Percentage believing that	Sex	Nudity	Adult violence	Child violence	Swearing, bad language	Blasphemy
Should be banned from television	23	18	14	27	24	23
Should be allowed on television with more restrictions	26	21	27	37	31	21
Should be allowed on television with some restrictions	35	40	38	22	26	33
Should be allowed on television with fewer restrictions	5	6	2	1	2	3

3

It is apparent that in these results there is little public support for any liberalisation of broadcasting in any of the above areas. Of interest is the feeling that more restrictions are needed on children's broadcasting. Naturally, any debate on mass media violence tends to emphasise the possible effects on child victims, and these will be of primary concern in later chapters. Nevertheless, the information gathered by social scientists on children's viewing patterns would seem to suggest that children invade the territory of adult viewing sufficiently often to make a distinction between children's and adults' television fare somewhat arbitrary for all but the youngest and most protected child.[5]

Of particular note is the number of people endorsing the most restrictive category of 'should be banned'. The use of this category suggests a fairly serious concern with the state of British broadcasting and a protectionist view of human vulnerability. There is nothing particularly unusual about the results of this survey — public opinion polls in the past have produced very similar figures. In Great Britain the responses to public opinion polls typically suggest that around 50% of people believe there is too much violence on television.[6]

With increased liberalisation of the arts there is obviously some basis for concern. During the last decade there has been a tremendous change in the type of material permitted in cinema films and on the stage. Richard Randall writing in 1968 argued.

... it can almost be said that anything censored as late as early 1960s would be licensed today, and almost anything censored today would not even have been produced for public exhibition as late as the early sixties.[7]

It is difficult for television to avoid drifting with this tide since it is so involved in the cinematic arts. This matter will be returned to in Chapter Two, when content analysis studies of television are reported. However, even though television may be becoming more violent, this in itself does not explain why so many people should express concern over violence on television when asked for their opinion by the public opinion pollsters. To partially answer this we refer to opinion poll data which attempted to gauge public opinion on the causes of crime and violence in society.[8] In this study an attempt was made to compare perceived causes of crime and violence in Great Britain with the results of a similar survey conducted in America. To do this the researchers gave respondents a card which listed 12 possible causes of crime and violence. Respondents were asked to rate each possible cause as being 'a very important cause', 'a fairly important cause' or 'of little importance'.

In terms of the rank order of the importance of the causes there was a high level of agreement between the American and the British results. The three causes perceived as being 'very important' by the most

4

respondents were: *General breakdown in respect for authority, law and order* (U.S.A. 74%, G.B. 58%); *Use of drugs* (U.S.A. 68%, G.B. 55%); *Laws that are too lenient or not letting the police do their job* (U.S.A. 64%, G.B. 57%). Throughout the results, the British respondents were more cautious than their American counterparts in agreeing less often that the causes offered to them were very important causes of crime in society. Interestingly, the only exception to this is *Violence in t.v. entertainment* where more British than American respondents said it was a very important cause of crime (U.S.A. 27%, G.B. 35%). This is quite ironic since American television is widely acknowledged to be more violent than British television — a view confirmed by the results of comparative content analyses.[9] There were three other causes covering the mass media. These were: *Theatres showing movies with violence and sex* (rated as 'very important' by 39% in the U.S.A. and 33% in G.B.); *Coverage of riots and violence on t.v. news* (U.S.A. 35%, G.B. 29%); *Coverage of riots and violence in newspapers* (U.S.A. 30%, G.B. 21%). Overall, the mass media are indicted fairly often. Clearly, a not inconsequential number of people feel that the media are a very important cause of crime in society.

Further, somewhat similar studies of public opinion have shown that there is an increasing concern over crime and violence in society. In these studies there is a pronounced tendency for the public to state the belief that the crime situation is getting worse.[10] One recent poll suggested that 75% of respondents believed that crime had increased over the preceding year in their own community.

To summarise briefly, opinion polls show that there is a high level of concern about violence in the mass media. Mass media violence is fairly often blamed for causing real life violence. Crime and violence in society are seen as increasing by the public.

At this point a note of caution is needed. Despite the apparent public concern about television violence, other evidence would seem to indicate contradictions. In many ways people maintain curiously ambivalent opinions.[11] This emerges in a number of studies, the most intriguing of which is a survey conducted in America as part of the President's Commission on Law Enforcement and Administration of Justice.[12] The particular study referred to, attempted to assess public attitudes on crime. Only 2% of respondents felt that the courts dealt too harshly with criminals. In other words, the vast majority of people were in favour of more severe penalties for crime. However, when these same respondents were asked how they would deal with a hypothetical youth caught stealing a car, the majority response was that he should be given another chance and treated leniently. Thus, although people have one opinion on crime in principle, they adopt a rather contradictory opinion when faced with a particular case. Public opinion polls on television violence have tended to measure people's opinions on television violence *in principle*. Perhaps a more meaningful image of public opinion might be obtained by measuring how the public behave when faced with particular cases of television violence. Here the data from the television companies is interesting. Here, as we may expect from the previous example, the viewing audience seems to hold a rather contradictory opinion to that obtained from the public opinion polls. Thus, in one period of study, in 1970, the ITA received 1 500 telephone calls commenting on programmes but only 3 of these specifically referred to violence.[13] Although it is in striking contradiction to the apparently high level of concern shown by the opinion polls, this data is much less scientific. People who protest to television companies may not be a cross-section of the population.

However, other evidence tends to support the view that particular cases are viewed differently to the general principle. Further, this evidence suggests that there is a discrepancy between public attitudes and private behaviour to the extent that while people may condemn television violence, they may actually enjoy it in private.

A recent study by Bob Roshier in England serves to illustrate the discrepancy between attitude and behaviour in this area and suggests one other possible reason for the apparent contradictions between the various data. Roshier examined people's perceptions of and reactions to the amount of crime depicted in their regular paper. The *News of the World* is legendary for its exeptionally high coverage of crime. Roshier discusses his findings thus:

Yet alone among the newspapers it (the *News of the World*) had a clear majority of readers who thought it had too *much* crime news in it. In addition, its readers were noticeably more critical of the way it reported crime, compared with the other newspapers. It seems unlikely that the *News of the World* has recruited among its readers a majority of moral crusaders dedicated to its reform. It is more likely that there is a discrepancy between what *News of the World* readers say they want from their newspaper and what they actually read in it. It also suggests that people feel guilty about what they themselves actually read in their newspapers, and that one of the categories they read and feel guilty about is crime.[14]

Of course, newspapers in particular and most media in general are sold in some respects like any other consumer commodity. It would be surprising if the manufacturers of these products were totally unaware of the opinions of their consumers. In fact there have been hundreds of market research studies conducted to date on the appeal of media violence to the media audience. The bulk of this research has been on the readership interest of various types of news items in newspapers. Here, it is clear that violent news items tend to be more interesting to the reader than non-violent news items. However, not surprisingly, this finding seems to be equally true of television programmes. The conclusions to the research have been well summarised in one recent review of the relevant literature:

There can be little doubt that topics of violence are of intense interest to the public and attract large audiences. The interest seems to extend across all media. It is somewhat stronger in boys than among girls. Among children it seems to increase somewhat with age.[15]

The belief that TV violence makes for high viewing figures seems to be an argument which is not uncommon among media personnel. The comments of Fay Weldon, author and television playwright for the BBC and ITV reflect this view:

Times are bad in films and television, producers and directors are frightened, they want to keep their jobs and violence is safe. For a start nothing is easier to write — it needs no imagination and a strangling is simply a good way to fill in five minutes *(The Guardian* 11.5.70).

The final chapter will discuss such considerations in detail.

So far, in this chapter we have discussed two images of public opinion. The one based on public opinion poll data apparently suggests a high level of public concern over television violence. The other image, based on public behaviour, would suggest the contrary, namely that media fare which contains violence tends to be popular. The conclusion is that the public condemn violence in principle but actually enjoy specific violent programmes.

We shall now consider a third image of public opinion, that provided by the mass media. As suggested earlier, the public debate reported in the mass media is likely to be the most influential on policy making, partly because it is so readily available and partly because of the importance of the people whose views are reported. The following discussion is based on press cuttings covering a period from 1968 to early 1973. Press cuttings dealing with violence came mainly from *The Times, The Guardian, The Sunday Times* and *The Observer.* The fifty items which appeared reflect both vested interest and political opinion. Since the media are vehicles for political agencies and other pressure groups this diversity is of major importance.

The observation made earlier that many television personnel feel that people are not really upset by violence on television is one which was also made by James Thomas in the *Daily Express* (24.6.68). This article referred to the censoring of television violence and suggested:

It is true that British producers, like their U.S. counterparts, are sceptical that the new anti-violence campaign will last. For a high section of the public is not adverse to violence, and when ratings are the most important factor of competitive TV, it will only take one company to bring out a really tough series for the others to follow suit.

There are a number of points raised by this. The first concerns the general issue of whether the public do or do not condemn television violence. As was suggested earlier, it is probable that people tend to condemn television violence in principle but not to condemn particular programmes. This observation tends to be supported by the press reports sampled. Out of the 50 press reports a total of four television programmes were mentioned specifically but only three were of the nature of complaints and one of these referred to a news item (*The Times,* 17.2.73)...

it is hard to see any justification for the BBC's recent transmission of the public execution in Uganda.

Complaints were levelled at *Tom and Jerry* and *The Avengers.* Mr William Price, Labour MP, asked that *Tom and Jerry* be banned since it was 'one of the most violent programmes on television' (*The Observer,* 3.12.72). *The Avengers* was criticised in the general context of programmes which may portray the infliction of pain as being both legitimate and enjoyable (*The Times,* 28.9.68).

The fourth programme which was mentioned during the period received attention in rather a more serious context. The headings to the newspaper article were 'TV dream may have led to fire death' (*The Times,* 24.1.68). This was an account of the coroner's inquest on the death of a Cambridge professor's son who was found with his clothes burning at his home. A few hours earlier the boy had watched a programme on primitive religions called *The Awakening Spirit.* The coroner said the programme had shown:

Vivid shots of men and boys dancing through the fire light and one shot of people walking through fire. I am told that the shots were in no way horrific, but it may be that the programme directly touched off ideas which led to this. In this case the boy got up, dressed himself and then for some reason it appears he soaked himself in turpentine and set himself alight.

This kind of evidence for the effects of television on its audience will be examined in later chapters. For the moment we are simply concerned with what the papers report on television violence. In this particular case, from the coroner's comments at least, it would seem that a non-violent television programme is being linked with a tragic case of violence. This makes the article somewhat difficult to embrace within the context of the debate on television violence.

When television programmes deal explicitly with violence then some censorship may be operated by the television companies. This is alluded to by James Thomas in the *Daily Express* article cited earlier. James Thomas suggests that censorship of violence is fairly common for imported movies. However *Z Cars* writer, William Emms made a fairly strong complaint that censorship was often practised without the author's consent 'quite often leaving the remains meaningless' (*The*

Sunday Times, 15.10.70). Formal censorship may be more prevalent than is often assumed.

Both the B.B.C. and the I.T.A. have established codes of violence which lay down guidelines for violence on television. These recommend certain restrictions on programme content, particularly for children's programmes.[16]

The former Home Secretary, James Callaghan, has argued that:

...if the B.B.C. and I.T.A. codes of conduct on violence were adhered to there would not be much complaint from the public ... (*The Guardian* 17.4.70).

Mr Callaghan asked Lord Hill, Chairman of the Governors of the B.B.C. and Lord Aylestone, Chairman of the I.T.A., to meet him for a discussion on what — if anything — should be done to restrict crime and violence on television. The I.T.A. was,

surprised at the invitation, since it operates what it considers to be a strict code of violence. It also claims to be particularly careful during the early parts of the evening, when children might be watching.[17]

Clearly the broadcasting organisations may be sensitive to public criticism, especially under the implied threat of government intervention. However, it may be difficult for producers to avoid violating those rules implied in the codes of conduct on violence. This is because the context of violence may be a crucial factor in deciding whether or not a given act of violence is unacceptable. This point was made in an article in *The Guardian* (9.11.70).

...it is obviously possible that a particular work of art may have bad 'subject matter effect' and 'good aesthetic effect' for instance, *Othello* might (conceivably) keep us awake at nights or even inspire us to jealousy and violence, whilst at the same time enlarging our understanding and perception. If and when research shows such clashes to exist, we should have to choose whether to put our money on education or (so to speak) on a quiet life.

The balance between cultural worth on the one side and possible harmful consequences on the other is not easily drawn. Nevertheless the above argument suggests an important subtlety which is notably absent in the press reports.

In the press reports sampled, it would seem that, overwhelmingly, the public reads accounts of television being blamed in one way or another for its coverage of violence. The sample of newspaper articles taken was classified very simply into the two categories of 'for' or 'against'. In the 'against' category was placed any statement suggesting that there was too much television violence or that television violence had harmful effects. In the 'for' category was placed any statement suggesting that people may like television violence or that it may not have harmful effects. The 'for' category was somewhat generous since it included 'balanced' arguments like the *Guardian* article cited above.

Despite the generous definition of 'for' statements, the sample of press reports showed that only 7 out of 50 statements fell into this category. Thirty-five statements (70%) were classified as 'against' television violence. The remaining newspaper articles in the sample could not be classified on this dimension since they were announcements of pending research reports and the like. Just over half (19 of the newspaper items) which were classified as 'against' were of a general nature. As suggested earlier, specific television programmes were very rarely mentioned in any of the articles. However, they were also general in the sense that the majority did not make any attempt to provide a reason for the statements. Two examples will suffice for this type of newspaper item. The first is an article in *The Guardian* (5.5.70):

Curtain raiser on TV violence

... Mr Callaghan at a foundation stone-laying at the Central Criminal Court, referred to the increasing number of crimes committed by young men. 'Some of us may wonder,' he continued, 'whether it is incidental this age group represents what has been described as the first television generation'.

The second article in *The Times* (17.4.71) began:

Mr. Trevelyan condemns film violence

Mr John Trevelyan, retiring secretary of the British Board of Film Censors, gave a warning last night of the danger of violence in films and on television.

If anyone enjoyed seeing violence on the screen, and got a kick out of it, that person was a danger to society, he told a British Federation of Film Societies seminar in London.

Although the 16 remaining newspaper items in the 'against' category tended to be a little vague, a fairly wide range of reasons were offered. Before examining these reasons, it should be noted that perhaps the number of analytical statements is not particularly low considering that the opinion poll data and that the balance of newspaper coverage of television violence is such that a condemnation of violence is perfectly respectable and does not necessarily require any justification. Nevertheless, just less than half of the 'against' newspaper items did offer some insight into the kinds of reasons for the views expressed.

The most frequent reason articulated was that television violence would lead to children imitating the behaviour shown. This category was largely made up of newspaper items which had what seems at first sight to be a good factual basis. There were two accounts of suicides which were attributed to the victims previously having viewed a television programme (*The Times* 24.1.68 and 30.8.69). Two of the newspaper items referred to the results of recent research which appeared to demonstrate that children may imitate the violence which they see on television (*The Times,* 18.4.70 and *The Guardian* 7.9.71).

Additionally there were a number of newspaper articles which used similar language to the quotation below:

> The Home Secretary, evidently determined to show that he is as bothered as the Conservatives about law and order, is said to have had representations from many viewers complaining that young people are incited to violence by what they see on the screen.[18]

In these cases it is not clear whether 'incite to violence' is simply a vaguer expression of 'imitation', or whether it is used in the sense of making the viewer feel more aggressive as distinct from imitating aggression. This last sense certainly provides a distinction which researchers have regularly made and which will be discussed in later chapters.

A further category of newspaper items which were classified as 'against' violence in the sample taken, was one which suggested that the danger of television violence was that it presented violence as something which was attractive.

The complaint by Mr. William Price, M.P. against *Tom and Jerry* is one such article:

> I frequently see young children enthralled at a cat and a mouse beating the living daylights out of one another. One can only imagine the effect this has on a young mind, the glorification of violence and the idea that it is all good clean, family fun (*The Observer,* 3.12.72).

This argument is similar to that levelled against *The Avengers* in *The Times* (28.9.68).

> One is tempted to think of *The Avengers* as television's best-boys' adventure story. But that is to permit the intrusion of a good deal of violence into a child's life and thus satisfy an appetite which we ought, perhaps, to frustrate.... what is unforgiveable — and television, abetted by indulgent parents, is often guilty of this — is to suggest that the infliction of pain on an enemy is both legitimate and enjoyable.

Possibly some of the concern expressed here is simply that it is offensive to see violence presented as attractive. Certainly some of the newspaper items suggested criticisms of television violence for reasons which appear to reflect concern over cultural values. Thus Fay Weldon, television playwright, was reported in *The Guardian* (11.5.70) as saying that she was

> ...not so much interested in any connection between crime and television as in the general debasing of social standards...

An additional reason for complaint over the presentation of violence as something which is attractive is hinted at by Julian Critchley, M.P. in *The Guardian* (4.1.71).

> ...television...by the 'approval' it bestows...acts as an accelerator to the growth of violent crime.

The mechanism by which approved violence is translated into a rise in violent crime is not specified by Julian Critchley. Nevertheless those newspaper items which draw attention to the 'approval bestowed' on violence by the media represent a useful step towards the kind of detailed observation which is necessary both to operate a code of violence and to conduct meaningful research into the problem of mass media violence.

As has been stated most newspaper articles were against violence on television and the majority gave virtually no indication of the reasons for the position taken. Of those which did give some clue as to the reasons, the majority were of a fairly general nature and referred, in the main, to the problem of imitation of aggression or that of the viewer being incited to aggression or focussed on the undesirability of television which portrayed violence as attractive. There were additionally a few articles which dealt with television violence in unique ways. These might be best described as constituting a small category of miscellaneous newspaper items.

One of these items in *The Times* (27.3.69) reported the results of some research under the headline:

<u>Link Between TV Heroes and Delinquency</u>

A link between the hero figures of television programmes and delinquency among teenagers appears to have been established by recent research into the effect of television viewing.

The hero figures were found to be particularly attractive to delinquent boys, while deliquent girls found prominent figures from the world of pop music most attractive.

Another news item, again in *The Times* (23.4.70), noted that Robin Day, anchorman of B.B.C.'s *Panorama,* believed a 'confusing paradox' existed over television violence.

While newsreel shots of death and violence, say, in Vietnam or Nigeria have tended to lead to a pacifist revulsion against war, conversely the presence of television cameras often helps to create an explosive atmosphere in what might otherwise be a peaceful situation.

This last newspaper article is an unusual one in containing both an argument and a counter-argument. Only one other item in the sample attempted any balanced discussion of the issues involved.

As stated earlier the great bulk of newspaper items were against television violence and yet did not offer very specific reasons for the position adopted. The minority of newspaper items which did not come out against television violence were of an equally general nature. The only exceptional case was quoted in *The Guardian* (17.4.70) when Mr Michael Barnes, M.P. asked Mr Callaghan to take care not to encourage some of the 'irrational prejudices' about violence on television:

Is it not equally possible to argue that, for many people, the spectacle of violence on television can have the effect of purging violent emotions? Cannot these things be safely left to the broadcasting authorities?

Two other newspaper articles which denied any effects of television violence were very bald statements:

There is as yet no solid evidence to link television to violence or a permissive attitude to sex, Lord Hill, Chairman of the B.B.C. declares.[19]

and *Z Cars* writer, William Emms claimed:

There was no shred of evidence to connect TV violence with the rising crime rate (*The Sunday Times*, 15.10.70).

Both of these statements occurred in the context of other arguments about television and so did not appear as the predominant point of the articles. This was the characteristic of the remaining newspaper items which were classified as 'for' television violence in our categorisation of the sample.

Three of these items had a broad approach as shown in the following quotation from *The Times* (27.5.71). This item was entitled:

Women find TV plays are not so horrid

It began

The notion that television plays are full of sex, violence and bad language was challenged by the results of a survey conducted among 200 women viewers in Northern Ireland who volunteered to watch 17 plays for the Independent Television Authority.

The article continued with details of one play which apparently received mixed reactions due to its sexual content.

The other two items which overviewed sex and violence have already been referred to. One was an article in *The Guardian* (9.11.70) which suggested programmes may have 'bad subject matter effects' but 'good aesthetic effects' and the other article (*The Times,* 28.9.70) noted that the I.T.A. had received only three phone calls specifically mentioning violence out of 1,500.

The final item which was placed in the generously wide 'for' category was a statement by a programme company chief in *The Observer* (29.3.70).

A programme company chief said yesterday "TV violence? Look, there is no more public disquiet this year than there was ten years ago. If anything, the past three or four months have been rather quieter than usual.

If you are looking for the reason Callaghan has intervened now, you'll find its origins in internal politics. The Tories come out with a big platform on Law and Order . . . What's the reaction? The Home Secretary takes almost daily steps — on drugs, supporting the police, and now TV violence — to make it plain that the Labour Party is as interested in Law and Order as the Conservative Party."

This last point is an interesting one because it draws attention to the problem that television violence needs to be considered in some context. In this case the author of the statement suggests that the reason for one complaint about television violence is to be found in politics. This may or may not have been true in this case but it would seem not unreasonable to believe that some of the newspaper articles which come out against television violence may have been promoted by reasons which may be peripheral to the basic issue of whether television does influence behaviour in society.

Context is particularly important in assessing the image which newspapers present of television violence. Although an overwhelming majority of newspaper articles condemned television violence in one way or another, this may be readily understandable given the function of newspapers. It is something of an over-simplification to suggest that newspapers only deal with the sensational. There are many reasons why a newspaper item should be newsworthy and thus worth printing. One of these is that a particular event is consistent with what we expect to happen — thus it has been argued that 'news' is in reality 'olds'. This argument seems to fit some kinds of news item — particularly perhaps those covering foreign news.[20] Here it may be important that the reader knows some history of the country before an event is understandable. Thus only national disasters and human suffering in that country will tend to be reported because these are readily interpretable.[21] Nevertheless, as *The Guardian* (9.10.71) pointed out:

> True, there's not much point in presenting only happy news (No maniacs in grubby raincoats assaulted beautiful stripper Beryl Scraggs as she walked home last night) but anyone who relied on the TV news for his sole source of information on the human condition would go quietly, or even very noisily, out of his mind.

For this reason news which condemns television violence will tend to be more newsworthy than news which does not condemn television violence. Potential news items on television violence cannot readily fall into a category of 'violence praised' or include items which 'exonerate television from all blame'. The most likely category for any supporter of television violence is one which, in terms of news value, is quite dull — namely 'violence not condemned' and includes items like those occasionally reported: 'There is no evidence . . .' and so on.

The way in which the psychological research on the effects of television was reported is interesting in this context. In the main, these items were presented as evidence in favour of the view that television violence is harmful. There were a number of news items with headings like 'Link between TV heroes and delinquency' (*The Times,* 27.8.69) or 'Television blamed for U.S. violence' (*The Times* 25.9.69). However, more revealing were the news items concerned with the failure to find any harmful effects. Pleas by researchers that the issues were not clear cut and resolved, or suggestions that more research is needed were

14

placed in the context of hostile criticism. Thus 'Death every 45 minutes — four TV moguls grilled' (*The Observer* 5.1.69) provided a conversation between Dr Stanton, President of Columbia Broadcasting Services and a congressman. Dr Stanton's comment that 'we simply don't know' was made to look somewhat naive in the light of information reported on the amount of money spent on advertising in America. The implication was that it was quite illogical to assume there were no effects of the mass media. Two other news items reporting ongoing research fell under the headlines of '£¼m. spending on report angers I.T.A.' (*The Daily Telegraph,* 10.3.69) and 'I.T.A. anger over "wasted grant"' (*The Guardian* 27.3.69). It is not clear what the ideal outcome of the funds should have been, but some indication is given by the comment in *The Guardian* that a report was expected from the researchers . . . 'However, its results are believed to be inconclusive.' Letters from readers on the research were more forthright.

Frankly I am a little tired of being told we must put up with all shows of violence till the sociologists or psychiatrists can measure the effects (*The Times,* 18.4.69).

The theme of a feature by Jill Tweedie in *The Guardian* (11.5.70) spelt out the reservations which seem to be implicit in a number of these news items:

Yet to my mind, a hundred thousand surveys will shed no light at all.

It should be stressed, however, by way of summary, that these reservations to and criticisms of the research were not present in reports of research showing harmful effects. They existed in those cases where some assertion was made that 'there is no evidence that television violence is harmful'. Of course without knowing the full range of news material available to the press on television violence it is difficult to know how far this apparent bias in newspaper coverage reflects editorial policy. Nevertheless the way in which newspapers cover the television violence debate is certainly intriguing. It is so for two reasons.

First of all the image presented by newspapers is one which is characterised by a negative reaction to television violence. The newspaper items sampled show that only a very small minority of articles cannot be classified as being against television violence. The second intriguing aspect of the newspaper coverage is that we cannot be sure how far the image presented by newspapers influences public opinion. It has been suggested by some researchers that the media amplify problems.[22] Thus, publicity given to violent crimes may lead to the police feeling that there is 'too much of it about' and prosecuting more people.

This leads to a 'rise' in violent crime. The judiciary and the legislature may react in similar ways. Naturally the public is not excluded in this process as their opinion may be influenced by reading that violent crimes are increasing — they may report more crime and influence MPs to press for more sanctions thus increasing the spiral of 'rising' crime. This phenomenon can only arise when a percentage of crimes typically goes undetected by the legal system. However, there is strong evidence to suggest that this is actually the case. Clearly many more women are raped than the police records would indicate and police prosecutions for drunkenness are hardly a reliable measure of the extent of drunkenness in society. More surprising is the degree of under-reporting. Overall the estimates suggest that only between 15% and 25% of crime is recorded as known to the police.[23]

At the moment there is little evidence to indicate what the relationship is between public opinion polls and newspaper coverage of an issue. Naturally newspapers perceive a potential readership for certain types of news item but this could simply be the 'cause' of a media produced effect of spiralling public opinion.

At present all that can be said is that newspaper coverage and public opinion polls both suggest a high level of concern about violence on television. There exists other evidence about public behaviour which suggests that the newspapers and the public opinion polls present a somewhat exaggerated picture of public concern and that in reality violence is not disliked in the media. It would be wrong to argue any causal relationship between these different images of public concern on the basis of available evidence, but it would indeed be ironic if the mass media themselves turned out to be an important source of public concern about the mass media.

CHAPTER TWO
MASS MEDIA VIOLENCE AS A PSYCHOLOGICAL PROBLEM

The mass media contribute much to modern life — if only in terms of the amount of time that individuals devote to them — and the question of their impact on society cannot be ignored by those seeking to understand contemporary human activity. Since, as we will see, violence of one sort or another pervades the mass media, it too is an important 'fact of life' to be understood by the social scientist. Some would question whether we should consider media violence as a social problem, however. To define it as such may be to assume its effects, and the review of research we will present suggests that there is no satisfactory evidence that mass media violence causes violence in society. Another way of defining a social problem might be to equate the term with public concern but, as we have seen in the previous chapter, there are grounds for suggesting that the public concern may only exist in the reports of public opinion pollsters.

There is an even more humbling perspective on mass media violence which should not go unmentioned. This suggests that in the total context of social problems media violence is of relatively little importance. After all, road accidents take many more lives each year than criminal murders. Since it is unlikely that any more than a tiny part of violence, even granting the most optimistic claims, is caused by the mass media, we need to hold the issue in sharp perspective. While considering the miniscule contribution that mass media violence is likely to make to the total range of problems facing society, there are reasons for arguing that the media/violence issue should receive some attention from social scientists. These reasons are certainly not proof of the effects of media violence and are largely superfluous to the key empirical tests of the hypothesis. On the other hand, they do put into relief much of what we have to say in later chapters and provide a context for understanding the issues.

The amount of violence on television, the amount of television viewed by the general public, the amount of violence in the other mass media, the claims made by violent individuals of the contribution of the mass media to their activities, our theoretical knowledge of the impact of the mass media, and many other reasons, can be put forward to enable us to understand the potential effects of mass media violence.

Despite the fact that our review of the research suggests that mass media violence does not cause violence in society, the rationale remains of interest in its own right.

HOW MUCH TELEVISION DO WE WATCH?

There is no doubt whatsoever that the mass media are a central part of our lives. Not only do most people consume a great amount of television each week but television, newspapers, and radio are primary sources of information about what goes on in this country and in the world for 91% of adults in Great Britain, according to a recent survey. Television occupies more of the leisure time on more days than any other activity at all.[1]

Of course, people are not morons 'glued to the screen' while watching television — they eat, drink, knit, sew, play games, talk, cat-nap, read and study at the same time. Consequently, any figures on the amount of time that people spend watching television are inflated estimates of the attention paid to television.[2] In the United States people, including children, watch television for at least two hours every day and this corresponds with the general estimates for Great Britain.[3] Not all this viewing entails watching violence, of course, but an American estimate suggests that one in every ten American adults watch more than four hours of fictional violence each week.[4] Such figures vary with social class and intelligence.

While Frederick Wertham claims to have studied adolescents 'who in comic books, movies and TV have seen more than 10 000 homicides'[5] and others have claimed that children spend more time watching television than in school, these figures are not as frightening or far-reaching as they appear. Certainly they do not necessarily mean that television is as powerful a socialising agent as the school, nor do they prove that the modern child is more likely to commit murder or condone violence than previous generations. Nevertheless these and other statistics draw our attention to a possibility that media violence causes violence in the audience. One might argue that a child could not remain unsullied by such an intense onslaught in the mass media, but it could be argued with equal force that people learn to live with so many potentially disturbing things in modern society that we might expect them to be able to cope easily with the threat of television violence.

Even so, the amount of viewing is in itself relatively unimportant and a more crucial question concerns what people see on television.

WHAT DO WE SEE ON TELEVISION?

There is any amount of evidence to suggest that the mass media emphasise violence. The scientific study of the content of the mass media is virtually as old as any other aspect of mass communications research. The Payne Fund studies of the early 1930s gave the content of cinema films considerable attention. Edgar Dale analysed 115 motion pictures and found that, even in those distant days, 59 of the films contained murders and homicides or, at the very least, attempts at the same. In all, 71 deaths by violence were seen. Black and white, morally speaking, were carefully spelled out, as the hero of the pieces was only responsible for 21% of these deaths while the villain committed 40%. Heroines were virtually unstained by bloodshed, being credited with only one murder in all. Foreman wrote of this set of figures and the not dissimilar figures for crime:

> When we consider the universality of a picture, its permeation of the entire country, its penetration into the smallest towns and even hamlets, how otherwise can this scarlet procession of criminal acts or attempts be described than as a veritable school for crime . . . ?[6]

Such statistics on motion picture violence appear rather tame these days. The more violent image of modern films is partly the result of changes in the function of the cinema since the advent of television, and the switch to fulfilling the needs of a young adult audience rather than a family audience. Clark and Blankenburg[7] have provided statistics on the violent content of those cinema films made between 1937 and 1966 which have been shown on American television. Over the years, there has been a slight tendency for films to be more and more violent. The violence content of these films varies markedly according to the year they were made and there tends to be a peak in their violence content every four to six years.

Content analyses of television in the United Kingdom and in the United States[8] have shown that violence occurs in most aspects of television programming. In a recent intensive survey of a week's television programmes in Great Britain it was found, if we exclude variety, music, and similar programmes, that violence (defined as physical or psychological injury, hurt or death addressed to human beings or human-like animals in cartoon films) occurred in 63% of all fictional programmes.[9] A previous study in this country in 1970[10] had revealed that 56% of fictional programmes at that time contained violence. Likewise news and documentary programmes contain a good many violent incidents. For example, the 1970 survey found that 89% of national news programmes, 50% of regional news programmes, 50% of current affairs programmes, 50% of documentary programmes, and 70% of all these programmes combined contained violence. The recent survey showed that 23% of news items in the national news concerned violence.

The position in the United States is not so very different. Studies in 1967, 1968 and 1969[11] showed that 80 or 90% of American fictional programmes are violent. While the rate of violent acts per programme hour tended to decrease over this period, this is unlikely to reflect completely increased public and political pressures against television violence. It is more likely to be simply another representation of the peaking and troughing in the amount of media violence over time since Clark and Blankenburg have shown that the percentage of violent programmes on television each year has shown no consistent upward or downward trend.

An important question is whether the amount of violence in television fictional programmes is lower than that for those programmes which are watched by, and designed mainly for, children. In 1961 Schramm, Lyle and Parker[12] wrote the following description of children's television programmes in the United States:

For the most part, however, the children's hour on commercial television is a succession of fast-moving, exciting fantasy, leavened with broad humor and a considerable amount of romantic interest. It is extremely violent. Shootings and sluggings follow each other interminably. More than half the 100 hours (we studied) are given over to programs in which violence plays an important part. Not all of this violence is to be taken seriously; the cartoons and the ancient slapstick films are intended to be funny, rather than exciting. Therefore let us disregard all the slapstick material, and look at the following inventory, which will give us some idea of the amount and kind of non-humorous violence available to children at the hours of their intended viewing.

In the hundred hours we are describing, there were:

12 murders.

16 major gunfights.

21 persons shot (apparently not fatally).

21 other violent incidents with guns (ranging from shooting at persons but missing, to shooting up a town).

37 hand-to-hand fights (15 fist fights, 15 incidents in which one person slugged another, an attempted murder with a pitchfork, 2 stranglings, a fight in the water, a case in which a woman was gagged and tied to a bed, and so forth).

1 stabbing in the back with a butcher's knife.

4 attempted suicides, three successful.

4 people falling or pushed over cliffs.

2 cars running over cliffs.

2 attempts made in automobiles to run over persons on the sidewalk.

A psychotic loose and raving, in a flying airliner.

2 mob scenes, in one of which the mob hangs the wrong man.

A horse grinding a man under its hooves.

A great deal of miscellaneous violence, including a plane fight, a hired killer stalking his prey, 2 robberies, a pickpocket working, a woman killed by falling from a train, a tidal wave, an earthquake, and a guillotining.

This graphic account of television programmes for children certainly suggests that violence is rife during the periods watched (or supposed to be watched) by young people.

It is often stated that 9 p.m. in Great Britain marks the hiatus between general family viewing and adult viewing. After 9 p.m., although not quite anything goes, the programmes unsuitable for youthful audiences tend to be most frequently screened. Violence, one would assume, would be far greater after 9 p.m. than before. In fact, content analysis suggests that this is not the case. *While 36% of the programmes shown after 9 p.m. contain violence, as many as 60% of the programmes shown before 9 p.m. contain violence.*[13]

Actually, even though such a finding seems to reflect adversely on the social responsibility of the British programming companies, it is probably a much greater embarrassment to content analysts than to media executives. The difficulty with the method of content analysis, as practised, is that it relies on sterile notions of people's perceptions and the public's concern about mass media violence. By defining violence as an intention to hurt or harm, it is impossible to differentiate between an act of violence in a *Tom and Jerry* cartoon and, say, the death of Caesar. It would be justifiable if the public objected simply to intentions to hurt or harm no matter the context but, as we will see more clearly in the final chapter, they don't. For example, we discovered one dimension along which ordinary viewers differentiate television content,[14] which we called a 'violence factor'. Programmes which people perceive as being violent are defined by such characteristics as: people are seen to be injured; people threaten each other often; and violence is necessary to the plot. Other attributes of such programmes are that they make viewers tense, the stakes are high, and that kindness is not often shown. The programmes reflecting the violence pattern were *The Untouchables, The Saint, Man in a Suitcase,* and *Professional Boxing.* Interestingly enough, not all the programmes which would appear to demonstrate high levels of intention to hurt or harm were seen as being violent. For example, cartoon programmes have been shown by content analysis as having the highest incidence of violence but our sample rated such 'violent' cartoons as *Tom and Jerry* as being non-violent. Obviously the content analyst seems to see the world rather differently to the television audience.

This is not to say that content analysis totally misses the point. It does mean, however, that it cannot be used as a tool for 'divining' the audience's response to television and other mass media violence. Since in later chapters we argue that vicarious violence does not increase the willingness of the audience to use violence, the results of content analysis tell us that at least this is not because there is no violence on television. Hardly an earth-shattering finding, but it should be mentioned that certain countries, such as Sweden, show very little or no violence on their television screens.

21

Content analysis is a little more sophisticated — though some would say not much — than our description indicates. Despite the fact that it defines violence quite differently to the television audience, some of the concern with mass media violence is in terms of the nature of the individual who does the killing, fighting, or maiming; his relation to the law; whether his aggression is rewarded; and so forth. Such issues can be tackled by content analysis without being over concerned with the audience's perceptions of the programmes. Gerbner[15] summarises the television world of violence as follows:

The world of television violence is a place in which severe violence is commonplace. The main characters are unmarried young to middle-age males who become involved in violent encounters with strangers. Violent encounters are often unwitnessed, but when they are, the predominant reaction is passive observation and non-intervention. Violence, regardless of the identity of the initiator, goes largely unpunished. The central role played by violence in this cold world of strangers and passive observers is to provide a successful means for individuals or groups to resolve conflicts in their favour or self-interest. Forces of law enforcement are undistinguishable from others insofar as they also use violence as the predominant mode of conflict resolution. Legality, in many instances, is not a relevant dimension or concern.

While some critics have gleaned the 'messages' about violence transmitted to the audience from such composite pictures, Gerbner suggests the following three questions need to be addressed:
1. Are the messages which are sent actually received by TV audiences?
2. Are these messages learned?
3. Can norms for violence implied in these messages be learned and adopted as the audience's norms for violence?

Clearly these are inextricably entwined with the question of whether mass media violence causes real life violence and answers can be deferred until we discuss the effects of mass media violence.

WHAT DO WE KNOW OF THE EFFECTS OF THE MASS MEDIA IN GENERAL?

One must exercise caution in dealing with the frightening figures on mass media violence secured by content analysis, and equal reticence is required in evaluating the relevance of established theory in mass communication research to the mass media causes violence issue.

Anyone searching the social scientific literature for sound, empirically based proof of the disastrous effects of television and the other mass media on violence, sexual behaviour, and the like, will be disappointed. While there are those amongst scientists who are willing to scaremonger about the effects of the mass media, cool, rational evaluations are rather rare. Not surprisingly, given the wide range of social contexts, topics, modes of presentation and audiences which the mass media cover, it is difficult to give a single simple statement which draws together our knowledge of media effects. The mass media deal with the important and the trivial, with things which concern individuals deeply and things which are of no personal relevance to members of the audience. Clearly one would not expect the mass media to change the voting behaviour of individuals if they were rabid Conservatives or Socialists, whereas one might expect the mass media to affect the 'floating voter' — the legendary 'don't know' of social research.

The major theoretical formulation of the influences of the mass media of the behaviour of individuals — Joseph Klapper's *The Effects of Mass Communication*[16] — although published in 1960, remains *the* primary source. Perhaps 'theoretical formulation' is too strong a term to describe Klapper's interpretations — he calls them generalisations — but they are far from being simple conjectures based as they are on a wide range of research studies. Typical of his concise style, Klapper provides us with a brief summary of his proposals. He suggests that:

1. Mass communication *ordinarily* does not serve as a necessary and sufficient cause of audience effects, but rather functions among and through a nexus of mediating factors and influences.

2. These mediating factors are such that they typically render mass communication a contributory agent, but not the sole cause, in a process of reinforcing the existing conditions. (Regardless of the condition in question — be it the vote intentions of audience members, their tendency toward or away from delinquent behaviour, or their general orientation toward life and its problems — and regardless of whether the effect in question be social or individual, the media are more likely to reinforce than to change.)

3. On such occassions as mass communication does function in the service of change, one of two conditions is likely to exist. Either:
   a) the mediating factors will be found inoperative and the effects of the media will be found to be direct; *or*
   b) the mediating factors, which normally favor reinforcement, will be found to be themselves impelling toward change.

4. There are certain residual situations in which mass communication seem to produce direct effects, or directly and of itself to serve certain psycho-physical functions.

5. The efficacy of mass communication, either as a contributory agent or as an agent of direct effect, is affected by various aspects of the media and communications themselves or of the mass communications situation (including, for example, aspects of textual organisation, the existing climate of public opinion, and the like).

23

Despite the tendency to equivocate or qualify his assertions, fundamentally Klapper's position is that, by and large, the mass media have no effect on the audience other than to reinforce existing behavioural predispositions. The key word is *reinforcement* for which Klapper offers no formal definition. He certainly does not use the term in exactly the same sense as those psychologists concerned with the process of learning. He does not say that the effect of the mass media is to increase the probability of a pre-existing act being performed — although sometimes he implies that this might be the case. What Klapper seems to mean is that mass communications tend to be processed by the individual in such a way as to either support, or at least not contradict, the individual's own behavioural or attitudinal position. For this reason the notions of selective exposure, selective perception, and selective retention, are important to Klapper's thesis. Selective exposure implies that the individual exposes himself selectively to communications which support his own attitudes; selective perception implies that the individual sees in communications only elements which support his own attitudes; and selective retention implies that he forgets elements of communications which contradict or cause embarrassment to his own attitudinal position. There is some evidence for each of these processes but they certainly could not account alone for the ineffectiveness of the mass media which Klapper claims. Other processes are important.

The most important of the restraints on the effectiveness of the mass media is the social support for the attitudes and behaviour patterns which an individual possesses. In social psychological research it has been repeatedly demonstrated that the social milieu (peer group, family group, professional group, and so forth) partly determines social attitudes and partly sustains them. In a sense, to change one's attitudes is to reorientate oneself to one's friends and other social contacts. To overstate it somewhat — one would have to betray one's friends in order to change one's attitudes. Obviously this intimate relation between attitudes and social groups applies only to attitudes and actions which are important to the functioning of the group. The doctor who thought it proper to have sexual intercourse with his patients, the Hell's Angel who believed that motorbikes were stupid, dirty, and dangerous weapons, and the American President who suddenly became an out-and-out Communist, are all individuals who would stand little chance of social survival in their established roles. On the other hand, social groups are capable of coping with a certain amount of attitude disparity within their midst and to some extent minor bantering and argument adds to group cohesion. (The Hell's Angel who prefers a Japanese import bike to a B.S.A. probably would not upset his comrades too much.)

The social model of attitudes, then, suggests that the social costs involved in attitude change might be very great and scarcely worth the benefits that the change might bring. The difficulty is that people do change their attitudes and do drop out of their social groups at times. The social model is best capable of dealing effectively with attitude constancy and it cannot explain change other than in terms of the individual's relationships to new social groups.

The psychological model of attitude change, which includes the processes of selective exposure and the like, deals with the inter-relations of the elements of the individual's attitudinal system. The psychological model regards the individual's attitudes as being partly supported and maintained in relation to his other attitudes. If any one element of this system changes, others may also have to change. The attitudes may be related to personality and various needs but the pressures against change, as in the social model, are great. Obviously the social and psychological models are not incompatible.

An important feature of the two models is the *salience* of the attitude to the individual's social and psychological experiences. A trivial attitude is one which does not threaten either of these systems. Although this is tautologous, it does point to the circumstances in which one would expect the mass media to be effective in changing social attitudes. The more a communication threatens essential social and psychological aspects of the individual, the less likely it is to cause change. Briefly, ego-involved attitudes are resistant to change.

It follows that the mass media should be particularly effective in creating attitudes on issues that are new to the individual insofar as these do not threaten the existing ego-involved attitude system. The empirical evidence for this is clear and the principle accords well with common sense.[17] In fact there is a vast amount of social psychological research which explores the parameters of attitude change in the area of non-salient attitudes and any social psychology text book will provide a thorough grounding in this aspect of the literature. The difficulty with these attitude changes is that they do not appear to result in behaviour changes. This is not surprising, as attitudes manifesting themselves in the individual's everyday behaviour would probably be salient and highly resistant to change.

Whereas popular opinion has at times regarded the mass media as all powerful bully-boys, capable of turning the passive user into an active antagonist of society, Klapper's review tends to substitute a rather tamer version of social reality. Of course Klapper's account is not as helpful as it appears, since it is impossible to know whether the mass media are capable of modifying an attitude towards a particular issue without actually doing research to answer that question specifically.

What might appear to be a trivial attitude to one individual might be profoundly important to another, as many a public house brawl will testify. The generalisations are important because they integrate a wide range of findings, not because of the precision of their definition and predictions. The advantage of being able to compare new findings with established knowledge in a succinct fashion is important.

This formulates the difficulty with the question of whether the media cause violence or not. Our inclination would be to reject the idea as being unrealistic since it contravenes Klapper's principles. Aggression would appear to be such a well-socialised aspect of life that, whatever the media preach, it would be unlikely that the audience would be affected. Parents punish their children for aggression, some peer groups have aggression as an important value, and aggression is rewarded and punished in the playground. However, despite such socialising influences, there is considerable variation in people's attitudes to violence. A particularly important dimension seems to be that of the social approval for different sorts of aggression. For example, an American survey[18] showed that, in general, people could see no circumstances in which they would approve of a husband shooting his wife, a public school teacher punching or beating a student, or a teenage boy knifing another teenage boy. On the other hand, they did approve of a parent spanking his or her child, assuming the child to be healthy and over a year old, and of a policeman striking an adult male citizen. Obviously aggression is both approved and disapproved according to the context and the nature of the violence. Since there is no universal embargo on the use of violence, it is always possible, to give but one example, that a context might be redefined by the mass media in such a way as to legitimise violence in a situation in which it would otherwise be inappropriate. This is one of the concerns of those who object to the manner in which the mass media portray violence.

Since the social scientist knows precious little about the learning of aggression,[19] it is difficult to rule out the mass media even though we could point to studies which emphasis subcultural and developmental causes of aggressive personalities and gangs. While our ignorance prevents us from totally refuting the media-cause-violence hypothesis, it does seem to be in opposition to our knowledge of the effects of the mass media.

It is, perhaps, as well that we cannot rely on theoretical notions to limit the research into the effects of mass media on aggression. Theories can be wrong, incomplete, and misleading and, of course, ultimately we are dealing with an applied question which deserves an empirical test. After all, if mass communications researchers cannot provide data to show that the mass media do or do not cause violence in society, whether or not this is mediated through a social nexus, then it is difficult to see what important questions they can answer. There is nothing intrinsically more difficult in the media-cause-violence issue than in the questions of the effects of the media on voting behaviour, buying behaviour, and so forth. After fifty years of research, an answer

26

should be forthcoming.

IS THE MASS-MEDIA-VIOLENCE QUESTION ANSWERABLE?

Answers are never so easy as questions. Whether mass media violence causes the audience to be violent is a deceptively simple question. The reasons why it is such a problematic area strike at the very methodological roots of social science and perhaps illustrate why social science has had comparatively little influence on society. The difficulty is enshrined in the difference between the question *'could* the mass media have this effect?' and the question *'do* the mass media have this effect?' Social scientists are highly skilled at developing experimental situations which are capable of answering the question *'could'* but answers to questions of the social reality involved in the *'do'* question are much more difficult. This is partly because *'could'* questions can be answered by experimental designs but *'do'* questions cannot be answered in the same way. A little diversion is necessary to make this clear.

The fundamental problem of most sorts of social research is that the things of interest or variables (aggression, conformity, imitation, attitudes, and so forth) can be affected by any number of other variables. The variable in which we are interested is normally called the *dependent* variable because its particular value or intensity depends on other variables, whereas the variables which determine this value are called *independent* variables. In certain circumstances what for one study is the dependent variable, may in other contexts be the independent variable. When we ask the question 'does violence in the mass media cause violence in real life?' the dependent variable is real life violence, while the independent variable is mass media violence. Obviously real life violence can be caused by many other factors than exposure to the mass media, including inherited aggressive predispositions, aggressive parental models, membership of cliques which value aggressiveness highly, etc.

If this was not the case and only mass media violence was capable of producing aggression in real life, the social scientist's task would be much easier. Just as blue litmus paper in the chemistry laboratory turns red in the presence of acids, so would the viewer turn aggressive in the presence of mass media violence.

Because of the multiple determinants of aggressive behaviour, the ideal way to tackle the question of the effects of the mass media on aggressive behaviour must make allowance for all the other possible determinants of aggressive behaviour. One could do this by equating individuals in terms of all the other possible independent variables which might cause aggressiveness, and then seeing how mass media violence exposure was related to aggression in the audience. The difficulty with this sort of procedure is knowing which variables are in fact related to aggression — omitting just one is catastrophic.

The obvious way around this difficulty — the experimental method — involves the concept of randomisation. Randomisation simply means allocating individuals to what we call experimental and control groups on the basis of chance as in the toss of a coin. If we take, say, thirty individuals and allocate fifteen of them to each group on the basis of chance, we can be reasonably sure that the differences between the two groups can be explained solely on the basis of chance and not in terms of any systematic bias in our selection procedure. Of course, by chance there will be some important differences between the groups just as we can get twenty heads in a row by chance in coin-tossing, but this is the most unbiased way of equating groups in terms of the whole range of characteristics relevant to aggression. Now suppose that we introduce a novel activity into the situation — say we allocate one of our two groups to a 'treatment' in which they are required to view a film involving a great deal of violence, while the second group is required to view a similar film but in which the amount of violence is low. If the business is stage-managed correctly the only difference between the two groups is that one has been exposed to a violent film while the other one has been exposed to a non-violent film. Any differences between the two groups in terms of their aggression can be explained only by the effects of the film violence or, at least, something to do with the difference between the treatments to which the groups were subjected.

Clearly this involves intervention in a situation which distorts the relation of the experimental design to social reality. Experimental and control groups just do not exist in the real world; they are abstractions designed to cope with the limitations on inferring cause in natural groups. Although one could compare groups formed on the basis of, say, the individuals who watch a lot of violence compared with those who watch very little television violence, in terms of their aggression, it is impossible to use this ultimately as proof of a causal effect of television violence on real life violence. The reason is obvious: people watch television for all sorts of reasons and these reasons may be related both to liking television violence and to being aggresive. For example, working-class youngsters may prefer television violence more than middle-class youngsters would and also tend to be more aggressive than middle-class youngsters. Therefore, if those who watched television violence a lot were also the most aggressive, one could not say this is the result of exposure to television violence. It is the variable 'social class' which brings about this artifactual positive association between television viewing and aggression.

Ultimately the problem of the artificiality of the experimental method cannot be solved. Intervention is intervention and the big question is whether this intervention is important or not. One typical way of tackling the issue of the validity of experimental methods — for this is really the crux of the problem — is to compare the outcomes of

28

the experimental procedure with observations of real life associations between the independent and dependent variables; the argument being that if a correlation between the degree of viewing of violent television and aggression in the viewer is found and if it is shown under laboratory conditions that violent films increase the willingness of the viewer to be aggressive, then our confidence in the causal influence of violence in the mass media is increased. While this seems reasonable, it will not escape the reader that it is far from perfect proof. We will return to this in later chapters.

Of course these difficulties are only obtrusive if we are looking for answers to the very precise question of whether the mass media actually do cause the audience to be aggressive. If we are only interested in knowing whether the hypothesis is feasible or a realistic possibility then the interventionist methodologies are appropriate. The two questions are very different. Halloran[20] has presented a relevant argument in a different context:

> ... the social scientist must ask questions about the statements which have been made on the effects of televised violence and which it is claimed are based on firm social scientific evidence. It is one thing to say that if there is any risk at all in portraying fictional violence then that risk should not be taken (a position not far removed from that adopted by some broadcasting institutions, e.g. Danish Radio); it is another to make statements claiming to have established the effects of televised violence on attitudes and behaviour.

While social policy can be formed on the basis of mere suspicion, this is certainly not social science. In this book this self-same problem recurs at many points and cannot be fully resolved. In a sense our central argument — that mass media violence does not cause real life violence — is more easily dealt with than the usual 'mass media cause violence' assertion. If one claims that a phenomenon cannot or has not been demonstrated under laboratory conditions and that correlational or field studies suggest exactly the same thing, this is less questionable than claiming that the effect has been demonstrated. The reason for this is simply that a psychological process which cannot be discovered under the advantageous conditions of the laboratory experiment is unlikely to exist under any conditions. The tropical plant which cannot survive in the conservatory certainly will not be found in the garden.

It would be misleading the reader to overemphasise the role of the experimental method in our analysis even though ultimately it is the sole means available to the social scientist of proving cause. It is part of our orientation to research to take all reasonable sources of information as the basis of our argument. The laboratory experiment is as fraught with inadequacies, albeit different ones, as the correlational field study. To some extent one methodology bolsters the weakness of the others.

Furthermore, we have tried not to discard studies in a search for the ideal study, partly because the ideal is impossible but also because drawing threads from a wide range of studies leads to an interesting synthesis.

HOW DO WE MEASURE AGGRESSION?

What do we mean by aggression? Obviously there are many different varieties of aggression and to some extent what is considered aggressive by one individual may not be considered so by another individual. Further, can accidents be aggression or does aggression necessarily have to involve intent or volition? Having introduced some of the conceptual difficulties we must make it clear that we have no desire to resolve them. Our aim is merely to discuss what we consider to be valid indicators of aggression for the purpose of the study of the effects of mass media violence.

It is easy to spend valuable time defining concepts too closely. Granted that aggression is not a unitary concept and that there are many instances in which it is impossible to differentiate between aggression and, say, playful behaviour, no amount of pondering is going to allow us to draw fine distinctions. It is more pragmatic to seek instances in which the general consensus would be apparent and use these as the basis of our description of what is meant by aggression. Physical injury and perhaps death obviously constitute one element of aggression and so does the degree of deliberateness involved in this, although one must acknowledge that it is sometimes impossible to know whether a physical injury was accidental or deliberate. The sort of aggression which is considered to be a social problem obviously tends to be limited to those acts which society in general evaluates negatively. For example, in the study cited earlier[21] 97% of American citizens can think of no circumstances under which they would approve of a policeman shooting an adult male citizen. Bearing these brief considerations in mind, it would be most convenient to regard aggression as an intention to hurt or harm another individual in the absence of socially approved justifications for that act. This is at best an inadequate definition, but one which limits our attention to those acts which would be described as aggressive by most people. Some of the studies we will cite seem to regard aggression rather differently (in some, aggressive behaviour seems to be equated with assertive behaviour) which makes their immediate relevance to the acts defined as social problems dubious.

Social scientists usually do not find it very convenient to study the whole range of any phenomenon and tend to concentrate on fairly limited aspects of it which serve as indicators of the more general phenomenon. Aggression has largely been studied using aggressive attitudes, known aggressive delinquency, peer and parent ratings of aggression, and the like. Obviously these are all different sorts of measures and it is unlikely that any pair of them measure exactly the same thing. After all, the child who is aggressive towards his parents may not necessarily be aggressive towards his friends at school. We must accept that aggression is to some extent specific and that what might be a good indicator of aggression in one context may be a relatively poor predictor of aggression in other circumstances. Since there are many sorts of aggression there can be any number of different measures of aggression which can be useful.

Perhaps the ideal procedure for measuring the aggression of individuals is to observe their behaviour in natural settings and code this according to a predetermined schedule. For obvious reasons it is rarely possible to record systematically the aggressive behaviour of people. The most important reason is that, despite what the mass media say, violence is far from a common experience for most people and one would have to observe for a long time before a sizeable number of violent acts were recorded. However, there are other reasons such as the problems involved in individuals becoming aware that they are being observed, which may well inhibit their activity. A clear substitute for direct observation would be to use the reports of an individual's close associates who have noted his behaviour over the period of their acquaintance. This is often adopted but has the drawback that it is never fully clear what factors are being taken into account by individuals when evaluating their associates. Since aggressive behaviour is often considered undesirable it may well be that the trait of aggressiveness is attributed to individuals who are unpopular. Alternatively, it may well be that individuals are unfairly labelled aggressive by a social group and this used as a basis for ratings of aggressiveness.

Psychologists attempt to devise tests which correlate with observable behaviour, the argument being that these tests can then be used as a convenient and economical substitute for actual observation. While the logic of this is impeccable, the practice is difficult. Even if a paper and pencil test correlates with aggression, it also correlates with a myriad of other things which may have nothing to do with aggression. It is difficult, then, to know whether any change on such tests is due to changes in aggression or changes in any of the other things with which the test correlates. The *incomplete validity* of these measures as measures of aggression makes their use dubious as diviners of the effect of mass media violence. Projective measures of aggression are those which operate by having the individual project his feelings on to other people or inanimate objects — the well known ink-blot test is an example. Often the subject is required to make up a little story about ink-blots, ambiguous pictures, and the like which are then used as measures of aggression. These measures share similar problems to pencil and paper measures.

The projective measure of aggression has been used in a good many studies of the effects of mass media violence. Most of the research of the 1950s relied on such measures exclusively. Perhaps a group of kids was shown a violent cartoon while another group was shown a non-violent cartoon and their aggressive responses to the projective test measured following exposure to the film, the assumption being that if the film increased the individual's aggressive drive then this would be manifested in the child's response to the projective test. This might be the case, but it is possible that the child uses elements of the violent film shown in the experiment as the basis of his response to the test without the film having changed his aggressive attitudes or propensity to aggression by one jot. It is also possible that the projective measure reflects the very opposite of the individual's true drive state — for example, it has been shown that projective measures tend to reveal highly sexually aroused individuals as having low sex drives because, presumably, people can inhibit their response on the test.

There is another problem and that is that we are largely concerned with changes in aggression whereas the validation of psychological tests tends to be a static procedure — the scores on the test are correlated with known aggressive behaviour in order to assess the measure's validity. Unfortunately, almost invariably we know nothing of the validity of a change in the test score as a measure of the change in aggressiveness of the individual.

For these reasons we have chosen to ignore a large body of research literature[22] which deals with the effects of exposure to mass media violence on projective and similar measures of aggression. The point is that since we have data which deal with more overt forms of aggression there is no need to bother with less relevant data with all their pitfalls. Certainly the literature using projective measures leads one to no firm conclusion on the media/violence issue.

PLAN OF THE ARGUMENT

While we reject the use of projective measures of aggression as satisfactory bases for the study of the effects of mass media violence, we have otherwise tried to take the widest view of the research which can be designated social scientific. We dwell no more on the experimental evidence than the correlational evidence but, of course, we recognise that certain research methodologies are better than others at answering certain sorts of question.

Chapter Three deals with experimental studies of the effects of media violence. Rather than confining ourselves to the purely laboratory research in this area a number of field experiments are discussed, as these shed a good deal of light on the generalisability of laboratory findings to more naturalistic conditions. Various artifacts of the laboratory experiments are discussed and evidence of their inadequacy provided. It is concluded that these studies say nothing about the real effects of media violence, and their status as a proven laboratory phenomenon is in serious doubt.

Chapter Four discusses the evidence for and against the various psychological processes which could bring about the effects of the mass media on violence. Attitude change, identification, triggering, desensitisation, and imitation, are all critically treated. There is little or no sound support for any of these processes being incriminated in the effects of mass media violence, which adds to our confidence in the view that mass media violence does not cause violence in real life.

Chapter Five introduces the wide variety of correlational field studies which point to the adverse effects of media violence on violence and delinquency in real life. Various artifacts are discussed in these studies and a subcultural theory advocated which integrates the widely conflicting conclusions of these studies and which indicates strongly that the mass media do not cause violence and delinquency.

The final chapter opens out the issue somewhat and discusses why the question of mass media violence needs to be understood in rather different ways.

CHAPTER THREE
EXPERIMENTAL STUDIES
OF THE EFFECTS OF
MASS MEDIA

Without doubt the bulk of laboratory experiments on the effects of media violence have been interpreted as clearly favouring the view that filmed violence increases the level of aggression in the viewer. It is equally clear that most experimental social psychologists who have researched the area are convinced of the media's adverse influence. However, this apparent unity glosses over a wide range of mistaken assumptions, dubious methodologies, empirical contradictions, and wrong generalisations which, when considered, help support the central contention of this book — that media violence has no effect on the level of violence in society. Given the consensus opinion of the researchers, it is clear that our contention involves, of necessity, a complex argument disputing the conclusions of many studies. We would argue, however, that consensus does not necessarily mean that these studies gel into a coherent body of knowledge. In fact, some studies contradict the general consensus and it is important to understand why this is so. Furthermore, many of the studies are based on such fragile procedures that their intrinsic worth may be doubted. Despite the consensus of experts in this area, by and large these studies have been uninfluential in determining public policy — partly as a consequence of the factors discussed in this chapter.

CATHARSIS OR STIMULATION
There have been two major suppositions about the effects of mass media violence. The first of these is that to see vicarious violence on film or television will 'discharge' the aggressive energy of the individual. This is called *catharsis*. While few would argue that *personally to attack a source of frustration* does not have this purgative function (an assertion for which there is empirical support), it is a very different matter to assume that to see a third party attack someone who is not the source of the viewer's aggression has this same function. In some ways to argue that media violence is cathartic is tantamount to suggesting that witnessing people eating when one is hungry will make one feel less hungry.[2] No empirical studies have investigated this but it would be surprising to find that 'vicarious' eating reduced hunger. This is, of course, not to suggest that experiencing aggression vicariously

cannot result in the lowering of aggression. Presumably to see a five-stone weakling attack a fifteen-stone bully and get beaten to a pulp would motivate nobody (especially other five-stone weaklings) to follow his example.[3] But this is hardly the same mechanism as catharsis since it involves the *inhibition* rather than the *discharge* of aggression — a point which should not be overlooked, as a very similar argument underlies much of the early research on the effects of media violence.

The other major supposition about the effects of mass media violence has been that it leads to greater aggressive tendencies in the audience.[4] There is no necessary reason to suppose that both catharsis and stimulation of aggression are mutually exclusive but it has overwhelmingly been found that film violence stimulates rather than reduces the amount of aggression in the viewer. It is notable that the 'no-effects' argument is rarely put by researchers. Our argument is that vicarious aggression has no causal effect on the level of violence in society — or, at least, that it has not been satisfactorily proven that it has any effects.[5] This is partly a question of the validity of the laboratory experiment but also one of its generalisability.

A key concept in the early history of research in this area is that of aggression anxiety.[6] A precise definition of this is unimportant but a description of its implications might be useful. Because we are taught that aggression, except in certain socially approved circumstances, is wrong, we tend to feel anxious at the prospect of acting aggressively. Such feelings inhibit us from displaying our anger, and the more this anxiety is aroused the less aggressive we are likely to be. Since socialisation processes inhibit unwelcome impulses rather than tell us how to avoid having them in the first place, it is not surprising that the two antagonistic factors can occur simultaneously. If the concept of aggression anxiety is useful then one would expect that aggression would most readily manifest itself in situations in which it is socially approved. In other words, the more an individual is presented with stimuli which reduce his anxieties about aggression, the more likely he is to aggress.[7]

The key proponent of the catharsis view in America has been Seymour Feshbach, while the strongest empirical and theoretical criticism has been offered by Leonard Berkowitz.[8] However Feshbach's hypothesis about catharsis contains several important qualifications:

> In order for an activity to have drive reducing properties, components of the drive must be present or evoked during the performances of the activity; that is, there must be some fractional connection between the vicarious act and the original drive instigating conditions. Otherwise if aggressive drive has not been aroused at the time of participating in the vicarious aggressive act, such participation results in an increase in subsequent aggressive behavior.[9]

35

Berkowitz argued that the idea of symbolic catharsis was unrealistic.[10] He suggested that an angered individual experiences a discharge of tension only in so far as he believes that the anger instigator or a close friend or acquaintance of the same has been injured or harmed by himself or some acceptable substitute.[11] These assumptions allow for the possibility that symbolic catharsis does occur, but in conditions so remote that they can be neglected — for example, if an angered individual was shown a film of his best friend beating up the instigator of his anger, this might be cathartic.

Feshbach carried out a study which indicated the feasibility of the symbolic catharsis argument[12] and Berkowitz's not unreasonable hypothesis was in doubt. Berkowitz[13] argued that Feshbach's study was complicated by the problem of aggression anxiety and that a decrease in aggressiveness in the angered subjects exposed to violent film was the result of the *inhibition* of aggression due to aggression anxiety and not the consequence of a *discharge* of aggressive impulses through a process of catharsis.

Berkowitz's basic experimental design to test his alternate hypothesis concerning Feshbach's findings deserves attention. There were six groups of subjects. Half of the groups were angered by an experimenter whereas the other half were treated in a more neutral fashion. One third of each of these groups were shown a non-violent control film, another third were put through a procedure designed to reduce their aggression anxiety and then shown an aggressive film, and the remaining third were put through a procedure designed to increase their aggression anxiety and then shown the same aggressive film. Finally, all of the respondents were given the opportunity to aggress against the angering experimenter.

The angering experimenter gave the subjects an intelligence test and, in the anger arousal condition, 'explained the test in an extremely condescending manner, and insulted the intellectual competence of students at the university while doing so'. He also badgered and insulted the subject as he worked on the test. In the non-anger arousal condition the subject was treated in an essentially equitable fashion. The next stage of the experiment was exposure to the appropriate film treatment. The control was a brief film about canal boats in England, while the experimental film was a seven-minute prize-fight excerpt taken from the Kirk Douglas film *Champion*. Whether or not the control film and the aggressive film were matched on all but the important dimension of aggression is a matter which will not concern us at the moment. Aggression anxiety was reduced in one group who saw the prize-fight film by informing the viewers that the aggression in the film was justified. They were told that the character played by Kirk Douglas was a 'heel' and deserved all he got. The other experimental group recieved instructions designed to increase their aggression anxiety. Kirk Douglas's improper behaviour was described as a natural out-growth of the harsh treatment he had received from others earlier in life and that he felt guilty about his behaviour and was about to turn a new leaf. Enough, one would think, to bring tears to the eyes of Berkowitz's middle-class, American University student subjects; certainly enough to encourage the arousal of inhibitions against approving of aggression in these circumstances. Finally, when it seemed that the experiment was over, a second (non-angering) experimenter told the subject that the Chairman of the Psychology Department at the University wanted to know his opinions about the experiment and gave him some questionnaires to fill in. Amongst others, certain of the questions gave the subject an opportunity to 'get the knife' into the angering experimenter if he so wished. Here was an opportunity to make an adverse comment about the experimenter to 'the boss'. These critical items were 'My attitude to this task might have been better if there had been another experimenter instead of Mr. — (the aggressive experimenter)' and 'If I were to serve in other psychological experiments I would definitely not want to be with the same experimenter'. The same questions were also asked about the non-offensive experimenter.

Taken at their face value, these results are impressive — at least for the first item. Those angered by the experimenter tended to make more adverse comments about him than those not angered. Considering the angered groups, there was no significant difference between the neutral (control) film and the less justified aggression film while there was a significant difference between the justified aggression film and the neutral film. Anger and film had no effect on the subject's response to the second, non-angering experimenter. The films had no differential effects on the non-angered groups.

In summary, it would seem fair to conclude from this study that the following conditions are essential before vicarious aggression could have influence on the willingness of the viewer to aggress:

1. The viewer must be angered by the individual against whom he is eventually allowed to aggress.
2. Aggression in the film must be justified and not arouse aggression anxiety.

Taken at their face value these conditions would scarcely lead us to the view that aggression is a major consequence of exposure to mass media violence. It is important to note that the arousal of aggression anxiety did not depress the level of aggression compared with that of the control group — this does not tally with Feshbach's findings.[14] It should be noted that the procedure used in this experiment (like those of most laboratory experiments) increases the tendency for the film to have an effect because it operates, in a sense, in a vacuum isolated from the many salient and inhibiting mechanisms of life in the real world.

At about the same time in the early 1960s another distinguished psychologist, Richard Walters, carried out research into the effects of filmed violence and produced somewhat different findings. Starting from mass media publicity of a murder which had ostensibly resulted from a youth watching a knife-fight in the film *Rebel Without A Cause*, Walters attempted to replicate the essential features of the case in the laboratory.[15] However, instead of using knifings he used a device described by Buss[16] to measure aggression — the aggression machine. The idea behind the apparatus is very simple but very important in that it helps the psychologist circumvent some, but not all, of the ethical problems of using aggression in the laboratory. The machine consists basically of an electric shock generator which is wired up to the 'victim' in the experiment. Usually it is the role of the subject of the study to teach this 'victim' some task - the electric shocks being merely a means of delivering punishment in what has been described as a 'study of the effects of punishment on learning'. Not only can this shock be seen as a punitive stimulus but it is also a measure of the individual's willingness to aggress, as the duration and intensity of the shock are decided by the subject. Its validity as a measure of aggression is suggested by the fact that angered subjects tend to give more intense shocks to their frustrator than non-angered subjects. The subtlety of the apparatus is that no shocks are actually given to the 'victim' since the apparatus includes short-circuiting provisions. Paid accomplices of the experimenter play the part of the 'victim'.

In the actual study two films were used — the episode from *Rebel Without A Cause* and a control film about picture making by teenagers. Various groups of subjects were used over a series of studies — a wider variety of individuals than the university undergraduates who have been used in the bulk of studies in this area. Before being shown the films, the two groups were about equal in the level of shock they would give but, after being shown the films, the groups seeing the *Rebel Without A Cause* clip tended to give more shocks than those shown the picture making film. This finding was replicated on the various groups of subjects and provided more support in favour of the view that film violence causes aggression.

While, at one level, there is an apparent unanimity between these studies and those of Berkowitz, anger arousal does not seem to be an important variable in Walters' studies since the subjects were not frustrated by the victim and aggression anxiety is ignored. It is difficult to see that a knife fight does not arouse aggression anxiety just as the boxing film seems to. Knives are highly distressing to young people and one would expect that the use of knives would be more negatively socialised than the use of fists. Essentially the two studies are not compatible in this respect.

A weakness of the Berkowitz design is that it did not include a condition in which the verbal manipulation of aggression anxiety (the

38

justified and less justified aggression treatments) was omitted.[17] For this reason it is impossible to know finally whether it was these verbal manipulations rather than the content of the film which brought about the differences in the willingness to aggress. This is not, of course, a difficult problem to overcome, but it does emphasise the magnitude of the task involved in integrating such studies. The fact that non-angered respondents were stimulated to aggress in Walters' study by the aggressive film would fit in well with Feshbach's view that films are only potentially cathartic when a drive to aggress has been activated and that, otherwise, they are potentially stimulating.[18]

ARE POLICY DECISIONS POSSIBLE?

There has been a substantial number of studies employing the basic methodologies described above — the measure using the shock machine being preferred in general to that using aggressive attitudes towards the experimenter.[19] Despite the practically universal agreement that violent films have a stimulating effect on the viewer's willingness to aggress, the basic problem of the subtle incompatibility of the results of one study with those of another is troublesome. Take, for example, the question of the effects on the viewer's level of aggression, following exposure to film violence and witnessing the unpleasant consequences of aggression. It has been suggested by some critics that one of the dangers of the sort of violence shown in the mass media is that the consequences of violence are not brought home to the viewer. Indians are shot down without any sign of blood and long, drawn-out fist-fights leave bodies unbruised, and so forth.[20] The media would be seen by these critics as glamourising violence by leaving out the gore — not an unreasonable hypothesis, even though others have suggested that we may become desensitised to violence by watching such gory details. It is an idea worth investigating.

There are two studies bearing on this question. Both were produced as part of doctoral work, but basically the two are in some disagreement. The first study, by Hartmann[21], is treated in some detail since we will return to it later in the chapter. The study was of the effects of instrumental aggression and pain-cues on the same sort of electrical shock measure of aggression as described above. One novel feature of the study was the use of incarcerated juvenile delinquents rather than university students for the subjects. The films were specially made for the study so that there would be the maximum relevance of their content to the hypotheses being tested. The films were as follows:

1. *Instrumental-aggression film.* The first minute of the film portrayed two boys throwing balls at the baskets in a basketball gymnasium. The remaining part of the film consisted of a disagreement between the ball players which ended in a fight — the camera concentrating on the aggressors' instrumental

39

aggressive actions such as their aggressive behaviour, verbal utterances, and their facial expressions. Every effort was made to avoid concentrating on any indication that the boys were hurting each other.

2. *Pain-cues film.* This began as the previous film but the actual fight coverage concentrated on the pain reactions of the victim such as his pained expressions, cries and groans. As much of the instrumental activity was avoided as possible.

3. *Control film.* This started as the others but instead of breaking into a fight continued with vigorous play.

Half of the subjects were angered by their 'victim' and shown one of these three films while the other half of the subjects were not angered by their 'victim' and then shown one of the three films. Then all of the groups were allowed to shock the 'victim' in the usual type of learning situation.

The amount of shock (its intensity X its duration) given in the different conditions varied markedly, and not just in terms of aggression arousal and type of film shown. There was a rather complicated relationship between the effects of the two types of aggressive film and anger arousal. Let us take the two arousal conditions separately in order to make the effects clear. In the *anger arousal condition* it was found that the subjects would give the most shock after being exposed to the *pain-cues aggression film,* as compared to either of the two other films, suggesting that cues about the suffering of the victim have a profound facilitating effect on the aggressiveness of angered individuals. For the *no anger arousal condition,* it was found that the *instrumental-aggression film* when compared to the control film resulted in a much greater willingness to shock. Whatever else these findings imply, they leave us in doubt as to the appropriate ways to deal with different sorts of media violence. What appears to be potentially the most dangerous sort of film to show to the angered individual does not correspond to the sort of film that is potentially the most dangerous to non-angered individuals. It also suggests that aggression-anxiety is not generated in the angered respondent by witnessing the consequences of aggression.

Goranson[22] has produced evidence which suggests that the effect of an unpleasant aftermath in films is to reduce the level of aggression in the angered viewer, compared to films with a more pleasant ending. The research involved exactly the same film as used by Berkowitz — the prize fight scene from *Champion*. However, there were complicated verbal postscripts to the film. Only angered subjects were used. Tape recorded instructions to the film-clip involved the sort of aggression justification procedure which Berkowitz had found to encourage aggression in his experiments.

In the postscripts to the prize-fight scene, two different variables were manipulated. The positive/negative film outcome conditions describe the outcome of the film in terms favourable or unfavourable to the protagonist, and the consequences/non-consequences treatment suggested either positive or negative outcomes which were either directly due to the fight or due to events not connected with the fight. The four conditions were as follows:

1. *Positive consequence treatment:* This describes how the protagonist is given an award for his bravery and sportsmanship in the fight which led him to being offered a good job in a public relations company.
2. *Negative consequence treatment:* Here the protagonist dies an agonised death following initial injuries received in the fight.
3. *Positive non-consequences treatment:* This is roughly the same as the first treatment except that he gets the job by other means than the consequence of the fight.
4. *Negative non-consequences treatment:* This is similar to the second treatment in that he dies an agonised death, but as the result of a car smash rather than as a consequence of the fight.

The willingness of the subject to deliver shock following each of these treatments depended on whether the outcome of the film was positive or negative, but not on whether the outcome was a consequence of the fight or not. Less shock was given in the negative consequence treatments than in the positive consequence treatments. While no condition was provided for evaluating the effects of these treatments on non-angered respondents, it is clear that the effects of Goranson's treatments are not the same as those of Hartmann even though they were designed to get at essentially the same variable — the effect of negative consequences in aggressive films on the willingness of the viewer to aggress subsequently. Goranson argues that differences in the subject populations used and differences in the extremity of the negative consequences of the filmed aggression can explain these findings but, at best, such explanations allow us to question the worth of these studies in helping us answer the real problem of the effects of vicarious aggression. Studies of imitation (dealt with in the next chapter) have suggested that vicarious punishment for aggression can reduce the amount of imitation of aggression in line with Goranson's argument but, ultimately, it is impossible to formulate social policy on such inconsistent findings.

To some extent the problem is to do with the highly specific stimuli used in these experiments but also the lack of realism in the experimental situations. We are not arguing for the mundane realism position (that to be useful experiments have to reflect real life in a one-to-one fashion) but that social policy can only be formulated adequately in the wake of much more robust data than this. It is important to bear in mind the history of the development of these studies before rejecting them as unimportant or trivial — their origin is essentially part of a theoretical discussion of the nature of aggression and its reduction rather than the applied question of the effects of television, radio, cinema, and the printed media on the willingness of real people, in real circumstances, to aggress following exposure to a whole range of aggressive media content. There is a point behind all these studies which is at least subtly different from the purpose of the decision-maker in society. Although the question of whether these laboratory findings generalise to the big wide world is not to be neglected, it is of paramount importance, when evaluations are made, to bear in mind that the rationale of the studies is not exactly parallel to the more worldly concerns outside the laboratory. Psychologists go into the laboratory to free themselves from the complexity of the real world and construct a reality which is useful for their purposes but not always equally useful to the applied scientist or decision maker.

However, the problems of applying laboratory results to the real world cannot be overlooked simply by justifying the original laboratory studies. For one thing social scientists have not been reluctant to apply their laboratory findings to the real world of policy making or advice to parents and, for another, where there is such a paucity of research we have to clutch at the few straws available to us if we have any faith at all in the relevance of social science to social problems.

Later in this chapter we will turn to some of the field studies which have dealt, experimentally rather than correlationally, with the relationship between media violence and aggression in the viewer. The essential conclusion of these studies is that mass media violence has no effect on real life violence. But such studies have problems of their own — particularly those revolving around their tendency to deal with current states of affairs and to be incapable of dealing with changed social conditions and, indeed, new sorts of media fare — which make reliance on the more flexible laboratory experiment still important.

If laboratory experiments presented a wholly coherent perspective on the likely effects of mass media violence it would be reasonable to argue that we could not afford to take risks and that we should avoid all of the suspect media fare. After all, social policy decisions have been made (e.g. cyclamate withdrawal) on the basis of less than complete proof of the adverse effects of certain materials. On the other hand there are important questions about artistic freedom which must be balanced against our social scientific knowledge. Further, since there is some evidence that exposure to vicarious aggression can inhibit the willingness of the viewer to aggress (even though the concept of catharsis is inappropriate) it might be considered that to avoid media presentations of violence would be to lose some beneficial consequences of mass media violence. The issues are complicated and there is no sure path between research and policy.

In terms of our own argument, it is not surprising that there is a big difference between the outcomes of the studies since we doubt the validity of the methodologies involved and have a modicum of evidence to support our position. The fact that the field studies tend to support our contention is fortuitous and gives us added confidence in our interpretation.

EVIDENCE FROM MORE NATURALISTIC STUDIES

The range of field experiments dealing with the effects of filmed violence is rather limited. Few studies of importance have been carried out. That it has been essentially demonstrated by these studies that film violence has no adverse effect on real life violence might be predicted from the results of a laboratory study by Meyerson into the effects of similarity between the filmed aggression and the subject's aggressive task on the relationship between vicarious aggression and the subsequent tendency of the viewer to aggress. Meyerson[23] found that where there was only a very weak similarity between the modelled behaviour and the subject's own aggressive task, filmed aggression had no effect on aggressive tendency; where there was a strong resemblance between the modelled behaviour and the subject's own task then the apparent effects of a film on behaviour were great — at least for subjects with a history of being unaggressive, otherwise there were no differences.

There are all sorts of reasons why this lack of generalisation should be the case but it is worthwhile discussing the field studies before drawing conclusions on the basis of this one study. Perhaps the most thorough of all these studies is that of Feshbach and Singer[24] which dealt with the effects of violent television fare and did not resort to using film-clips. The problem with the use of actual television programmes as they are broadcast lies in establishing experimental and control groups on the basis of television exposure. Under natural conditions people may expose themselves to mass media aggression other than in random fashion and, if one found that those watching the most violent fare displayed more aggressive behaviour, the problems of knowing whether it was exposure that caused aggression or whether it was other factors such as the preference of aggressive individuals for aggressive entertainment which caused the correlation, are insurmountable. For this reason it is essential in such a study to allocate individuals randomly to either a violence viewing group or to a non-violence viewing group.

The way in which the researchers went about their task is interesting. Because they wanted to retain maximal control over the viewing behaviour of their subjects, it was decided to carry out the study in an institutional context since this allowed checks on viewing behaviour to be more adequately carried out than if the subjects were living at home. The sites chosen included residential private schools, boys' homes, and coeducational schools. Thus both the working class and middle class child were included in the study. A vast array of personality, attitude, behaviour, and television evaluation data was collected during the course of the experiment and it is a particularly notable feature of the study that the researchers concentrated on both aggressive overt behaviour and aggressive covert behaviour (fantasy).

There was a considerable amount of freedom in the sorts of programmes that the boys could watch within these broad categories, although they had to confine themselves to either essentially aggressive or non-aggressive TV fare (according to which group they had been randomly assigned). The aggressive programmes included *Bonanza, I Spy, Legend of Jesse James, Marshal Dillon, Rifleman, Untouchables, Virginian,* and *Wyatt Earp.* The non-aggressive programmes included *My Favorite Martian, Smothers Brothers, Walt Disney's Wonderful World of Color, Wide World of Sports, Lassie, Flintstones, Beverly Hillbillies,* and *Dick Van Dyke Show.* In order to minimise the danger that the control group would be frustrated by exposure to all this non-aggressive fare, which was slightly less popular than the aggressive fare, several procedures were instigated. Firstly, the child was allowed to opt out of the experiment at any time, if he so wished. Secondly, most of the children were promised a fairly considerable sum of money to take part so that discontent with the restrictions of the experiment would be reduced; and when a minor revolt occurred in certain institutions due to the control group not being allowed to watch the television programme *Batman,* the researchers relented and allowed the children in the control group to watch this 'aggressive' programme.

Unlike most laboratory studies which have shown just a few minutes of film as the violent stimulus, Feshbach and Singer's study lasted for six weeks and the children, of course, in that time watched a lot of television. Again, in sharp contrast to most laboratory studies, overt aggression was measured by ratings of observers (peers and those in authority) rather than by a contrived arrangement such as the aggression machine. Given that the study does involve a considerable number of possibly confounding events, as it stands it is one of the few studies that approach naturalistic conditions while retaining an element of experimental control. The study was naturalistic, of course, only in its use of real television fare, natural social groups, and measure of aggression in the real world. It is difficult to consider filling in programme ratings after every programme, watching programmes from a prescribed list, and so forth, as natural viewing behaviour. On the other hand, there is no reason to suppose that it is any less naturalistic than being interviewed by a correlational-study interviewer about one's 'typical' viewing habits. The possibilities of indirect and unobserved measurement in social science are, unfortunately, rather limited.

44

The behaviour and fantasy of the boys was monitored continuously throughout the period of the experiment. Although there was a certain amount of inconsistency in the results obtained from different schools and different sub-groups of the population studied, broadly speaking the results give a picture favourable to the hypothesis that exposure to vicarious violence does not amplify the willingness of the viewer to engage in overt violent activity. This is in terms of aggression against peers and those in authority as measured by reports made by these people. In fact, if anything, the results suggested that vicarious aggression has a *beneficial* effect upon the level of violence in the viewer since there was a tendency for the aggression ratings to be significantly lower for the experimental group than for the control group not exposed to the violent television diet.

A finding which supports our decision not to consider studies of the effects of vicarious aggression on projective measures of aggression was that measures of fantasy aggression (as measured by the Thematic Apperception Test — commonly used in the projective studies in this area) tended to indicate the very opposite to the behavioural measures. That is, the control group tended to give the *least* aggressive responses to the fantasy measure while the experimental group tended to give the *most* aggressive responses. This clearly indicates that projective and behavioural aggression are very different things and that one cannot assume a positive relationship between the two. Interestingly enough, measures of the effects of exposure on attitudes to violence tended to conform more to the behaviour indexes rather than to the fantasy measures — a point worth remembering when considering the discussion of the effects of vicarious aggression on aggressive attitudes presented in the next chapter.

It will not have escaped the reader that there are any number of possible artifacts associated with the above study. Some of these have been discussed in the literature and to some extent answered.[25] Apart from such questions as the problems of differential likings for the two different sorts of media fare, it is difficult to evaluate what sorts of rumours might have been generated in the institutions to explain the rather strange antics of the researchers. Although Feshbach and Singer go to considerable pains to point out that as far as they know the prevalent assumption in the institutions about the effects of television violence was that it had no effect or had a stimulating effect, we have no ultimate way of knowing that this would bias the results of the study in the opposite direction to the actual findings. If individuals thought that the experimenters expected the experimental group to demonstrate a higher level of aggression than the control group there is no necessary reason to suppose that those involved would act in accordance with this hypothesis. Indeed they might make efforts to counter such an influence. For example, if they did not want the school to get a reputation that the boys were aggressive and easily influenced by television it would be an easy matter to ascribe the bad behaviour to the control group rather than the experimental group, thus producing the negative effects found. There is a certain amount of laboratory evidence to suggest that respondents who perceive the purpose of an experiment do not necessarily act to support these perceptions.[26]

William D. Wells[27] replicated the study by Feshbach and Singer in essential details. However, his results, in general, were not supportive of most of the original conclusions. By and large, no consistent pattern emerged in this study which really meets the no-effects thesis rather than the stimulation or catharsis arguments. Wells sees slight trends in his data which tend more to support stimulation but the tone of the report is one of despair of the methodology rather than of conviction. This conclusion is very much in line with that of Ball-Rokeach[28] in her review of the Feshbach and Singer study. She wrote:

> The majority of the experimental results show no significant differences in aggressive behaviour between experimental and control subjects. Thus there is little in the way of research evidence which supports the catharsis hypothesis.

The results of these experiments certainly do not impress one with a sense of the adverse effects of media violence.

There have been other studies which have used rather younger children than in the above cases. However these have used filmed material rather than actual television programmes and real life overt aggression as the dependent variable. Stein and Friedrich[29] took as their subjects 3 — 6 year old pre-school children in a University nursery school. The children came from a wide variety of home backgrounds and the poor were not excluded simply on the basis of their inability to pay for the schooling. Trained observers were used to rate the behaviour of the children prior to the repeated exposure to one of three different sorts of films — aggressive, neutral, or pro-social (which emphasised constructive and commendable behaviour) — in order to assess baseline frequencies of different sorts of aggressive and pro-social behaviour. Behaviour was monitored during free play observation periods for the four weeks of the experimental period and also during the two weeks following this experimental period. The change in different sorts of aggression between the time prior to the films being shown and the period immediately following film exposure was the measure of the effects of the film. Stein and Friedrich used two different sub-groups of children — those highly aggressive in the pre-film period and those low on aggression during the pre-film period. Only in the highly aggressive groups for one of the measures of aggression did they find any differences which could be attributed to the aggressive film.

A little diversion is necessary at this point in order that the findings can be understood. This is to do with the effects of pre-selecting individuals to be high or low on a variable (aggression in this case) on the scores on the same variable at a later retesting. In fact, what happens in such cases (given that the variable being measured cannot be perfectly assessed by the measuring instrument — which is the case with all psychological measures) is that there is a tendency for the group initially high on the variable, on retesting to become lower, and those initially low on the variable to become higher on retesting. There is nothing magical about this — it is simply a statistical fact of life for unreliable measuring instruments. A coin-tossing example will serve to illustrate the phenomenon. If we flip a coin we are engaging in what is assumed to be a chance procedure. We expect that the heads and tails will each fall uppermost in 50% of the instances over the long run.

If we took 24 pennies and tossed them we would expect, by chance, 12 to land heads and 12 to land tails. If we pick up the 12 coins that landed heads and call them the 'heads' group and form the 'tails' group in a similar fashion and again toss these sets of coins we do not expect all of the coins in the heads group to land heads and all of the coins in the tails group to land tails. We expect, by chance, 6 heads in the tails group and 6 tails in the heads group — our groups having 'regressed to the mean'. Because the toss of a coin does not predict at all the behaviour of a coin on the next toss, regression to the mean is complete. Where there is some relationship between measurement A and the later measurement B in pre-selected groups, the tendency for regression to the mean is not so great but it is still operative. The extent of the regression is directly determined by the reliability of the measuring procedure.

Regression to the mean was clearly operative in Stein and Friedrich's experiment. Those groups initially highly aggressive and exposed to the violent film regressed to the mean less than the similar group exposed to the neutral film, on their measure of interpersonal aggression. There were no effects due to the different films alone and no significant differences for other measures of aggression.

It has been suggested that the results of the study are due to the failure to match the different groups sufficiently precisely on initial aggression. Unless this is done it is likely that the groups will regress to the mean at rather different rates without there being any true experimental effect. This would explain why aggressive children regress to the mean less after watching violent films in the Stein and Friedrich study. It appears that this was indeed the case, since when the groups were matched for initial aggression, the differences between the groups became insignificant.[30] However, Friedrich and Stein in their later report maintain their argument by selecting groups which yield estimates of error variance small enough to produce a new significant difference. This is at best a dubious procedure.

A further difficulty is that there appeared to be scant consideration as to whether the behaviour classified as aggressive was in fact 'play' behaviour. There is little doubt that the mass media portrayal of violence can influence the child's play following exposure, but it can be seriously questioned whether this play behaviour generalises to beating up friends and old ladies. Stein and Friedrich included a fantasy aggression rating in their observation schedule, but the instructions to their observers seem to suggest that only cases in which the behaviour was clearly *playful* was it scored as such. Their definition of playful and fantasy aggression was *'aggression occuring as part of role playing or aggression in clear playful way. Conservative scoring here. (If in doubt, don't score.)'* which might imply that unless behaviour was *clearly* playful then it was recorded as real aggression. The social problem of violence would demand that the researchers only code things as aggression where there was absolutely no indication that the behaviour might be playful — quite the opposite strategy to the one adopted. The fact that behaviour was monitored during periods of *free play* only emphasises the problem.

Any rating methodology is beset with these and similar problems. It seems very important to define the distinction between natural aggression and playful aggression in the coding categories of any observational schedule. This might go some way to suggesting an hypothesis that where there are circumstances in which it is possible to confuse play behaviour with 'true' aggression that the film violence might seem to have an effect, otherwise there will be no effect. This might explain why Steuer, Applefield, and Smith[31] found effects of filmed aggression on the aggressivenesss of pre-school children in a free play situation, whereas Hapkiewicz and Roden[32] found no effects for six to eight year olds using a situation which encouraged aggressive competition.

The importance of this distinction between play aggression and true aggression is perhaps rather obvious and yet even the most recent experimental field studies are sadly wanting in this respect. Researchers at the University of Wisconsin have carried out two field studies in America[33] and one in Belgium[34] which seem to indicate an adverse effect of film violence. In both countries institutionalised adolescents were shown either a diet of aggressive films or neutral films for one week. Observers recorded the behaviour of the children before, during, and after the film treatments. Although the various research reports available do not give sufficient detail of the observational method, at least some inadequacies are clear. The behavioural measure is referred to rather grandly as a 'non-hierarchical, minimally inferential, time-sampling observational procedure'. Essentially it focused on aggressive behaviour and 'playful as well as malicious attacks were scored identically'.[34] Our doubts as to the relevance of this research to violence in society are further increased by the examples given of the behavioural categories. Thus, of the thirteen categories available to the observers, social interaction activity covers ping-pong, pool and basketball; physical threat covers fist waving, threatened slaps, and chasing; and physical attack covers hitting, slapping, choking or kicking. The crucial aggression categories therefore are quite suitable for describing an active game of basketball. Further, it seems that the raters may have been aware of whether the boys had seen aggressive films or neutral films. In Wells' study it was found that the rater's awareness of this to some extent explained the minor relationships found in this study. We need then to be very cautious in interpreting such data.

Alberta Siegal[35] studied the effects of violent film on the rated aggressive behaviour of nursery school children. Originally the study was conceived in the catharsis mould but the actual findings were insignificant and slightly in the opposite direction to that predicted. Each of the children served as his own control (that is, he took part in both the experimental and control conditions but, of course, at different times in the study).

Care was exercised to match the films on as many irrelevant variables as possible. A *Woody Woodpecker* film was the aggressive stimulus whereas the control, non-aggressive film, was *The Little Red Hen.* Observers' ratings of each child showed that interest in each of the films was roughly the same, which indicates success in matching the film treatments and may account for the null-effects found in this study compared to those in which matching was not achieved.

The observers coded the behaviour of the children following exposure to the film into several categories including the intensity and frequency of aggression shown towards another child, a toy, or to the self, and also rated the amount of anxiety demonstrated. The observer did not know to which group the child belonged, and so the ratings of aggression could not have been influenced by the knowledge of the sort of film shown. The aggressive film did not increase aggressive activities although it did cause greater anxiety than the control film.

Since there was a very substantial correlation between the aggression scores in the experimental situation and the child's teachers' assessment of the normal aggressive habits of the child in nursery school, it seems that the films could scarely have affected the child's normal aggressive behaviour. This study would cause us little alarm over the effect of aggressive film material. Young children might be expected to be the group most easily swayed by the content of films but here there is no evidence of the undesirable influence of the violent film. Certainly it provides us with more evidence that the results of laboratory studies cannot be generalised to real life without serious risk of error.

This is very much in line with the findings of experimental studies in other areas of mass communication research. There are any amount of attitude change studies which indicate that people can be persuaded to adopt a particular attitude on a particular issue, but the evidence suggests that only trivial aspects of behaviour can be influenced in this way and that issues relevant to the individual are not easily changed by any type of persuasion. The evidence for this is clearly put forward by Klapper, and this limitation helps us to understand the likely true role of the media in society.[36] The reasons for the relative powerlessness of the media are many, but the primary one stems from the fact that since most salient forms of behaviour are learned through interaction with other people — including peers, parents and the like — it is easier to change these behaviours by changing the social interactions of individuals than by enveloping them in mass communications. This is not to say that the mass-media cannot have a profound influence on the attitudes and behaviours of people, but only that they cannot really hope to compete with the real world on issues to which the real world is relevant. It is far easier, for example, for the mass media to convince the people of London that the people of India should adopt the modern agricultural methods than it is for the mass media to encourage the people of India to adopt these modern methods. Actual experience is much more effective than mass media persuasion, with respect to most issues.

The final proof of what is causing the difference between the results of field studies and the laboratory studies is difficult to establish and any explanation of the difference, to some extent must be conjecture. For example, the experimenter would have to spend a long time in his laboratory before he would see one of his subjects strike another, and he would have to spend a lot of time in the field setting before he would find the individuals administering electric shocks to each other for answering questions incorrectly. One has to concentrate on behaviours which have a high likelihood of occurrence, before experimentation and scientific study are feasible. That is partly why the laboratory experiment uses measures of aggression which are based on an aspect of behaviour that the researcher has encouraged and why field studies concentrate on reprehensible actions.

Given the radically different findings of laboratory experiments compared with field studies, the question of what overall conclusions can be drawn is not an easy one to answer. Certainly to the extent that the field study deals with the actual content of the mass media (as in Feshbach and Singers' study) it would be reasonable to conclude that our usual daily dose of media violence is not 'dangerous'. However, this could not apply to the findings of Siegel and others whose studies, while in a sense dealing with realistic measures of aggression, did not use normal media fare. Let us pursue some of the possible explanations of the discrepancy between field and laboratory studies.

The most obvious explanation is that in the laboratory experiment aggression is actually encouraged by the experimenter who asks the subject to fill in aggression scales or to deliver an electric shock — the only task for the subject is to determine how much shock or how unfavourable an attitude he should express. The aggressive behaviour in the real life study is not of this order. Aggression against a peer is for the vast majority of individuals adversely socialised.

A second explanation is that the naturalistic studies used rather more complex media material than the laboratory studies and that this complex material presented no unequivocal message about the use of aggression. This is a distinct possibility since the laboratory studies have tended to use snippets of film whereas the field studies have tended to use complete films or series of complete films. Unfortunately the distinction between the types of material used for the two sorts of study is very rigid and it is impossible to find any empirical evidence for or against this second explanation.

A third explanation of these findings is that some or all of the studies are subject to flaws and that the pattern of results obtained is an artifact of improper methodologies. The range of alternative explanations here is enormous. It might be that the field study is adequate and the effects found in the laboratory are design artifacts, or it might be that the laboratory adequately represents the true state of affairs and the field experiment is artifactual, or it might be that the two different kinds of study are subject to rather different artifacts, but artifacts just the same.

It is on the possible artifactual nature of the laboratory experiment upon which we concentrate since this is where our empirical evidence lies.

ARTIFACT IN LABORATORY STUDIES OF THE EFFECTS OF MEDIA AGGRESSION

There are two major sources of artifact in experimental designs — experimenter effects and demand characteristic effects. Experimenter effects, by and large, are the results of social interaction taking place in the laboratory study. It is always possible for the researcher to treat the subjects in his experimental and control groups differently (perhaps he appears more encouraging to the experimental group compared with the control group) which results in an apparent experimental effect which is in actuality the result of the differential treatment of the subjects on a basis other than that formally implied by the experimental treatment. This sort of artifact is essentially outside the scope of the available evidence on the effects of filmed violence.[37]

The other major source of artifact is much more relevant to the issue at hand. The idea of demand characteristics, suggested by Orne,[38] is that the very structure or technology of the experiment gives powerful cues as to the behaviour that the subject should exhibit in the experiment. This is unlike experimenter effects in that the emphasis is not on the interpersonal aspect of the experimental situation but on the actual design of the experimental procedures. The classical example of this is in sensory deprivation experiments where individuals are placed in an environment which is entirely devoid of noise, light, tactile stimulation, and so forth. This produces some fairly drastic effects on the behaviour of the individual and some studies have found that the respondents quickly feel the need to extricate themselves from the experimental situation. However, this is very largely a function of whether a 'panic button' (an alarm button the pressing of which indicates that the individual wants to be removed from the experimental situation) is present or not! If the panic button is present the individual tends to panic more readily than if such a button is absent; thus it may be the structural attribute of having a panic button available which produces the behaviour rather than sensory deprivation in itself.[39]

It is not so easy as one would think to discover whether it is true experimental effects or demand characteristics which are operating in any given experimental situation. The post-experimental interview in which the individual is given the opportunity to express his ideas of what the experiment was about would seem to be, at face value, an adequate solution to this problem. However, this solution is fraught with difficulties. These arise from the fact that these interviews occur *after* the subject might have acted in accordance with his expectations of what the experimenter thought the experiment would show. If the subject had acted 'improperly' by adopting any of the behaviours implied by these cues it is rather doubtful that he would express his true feelings during the post-experimental interview, since this would reveal his willingness to 'cheat' or to lead the experimenter on, rather than to act honestly as the subject of a scientific experiment supposedly should.

There is a certain amount of evidence to suggest that the post-experimental interview is a very poor technique for elucidating the possible artifacts of the experiment. For example, researchers have ensured that their experimental subjects are aware of the purpose of an experiment by having confederates pose as subjects and inform the real subjects what the purpose of the experiment was before they took part in the experiment. Post-experimental interviews probing the subjects about the purpose of the experiment were rather unsuccessful in persuading them to divulge what the purpose of the experiment in fact was.[40] In many ways this is not surprising, since the social psychological experiment frequently takes place in rather odd circumstances. For example, often the subjects are students on the psychology course that the experimenter teaches and they take part in the experiment because it is stipulated that a certain amount of experience in experiments is necessary before a degree in psychology is finally awarded. In these conditions one would expect the subject to feel constrained not to reveal everything he suspects. There is evidence to suggest that those with a minimum amount of experience with psychology courses behave rather differently in experiments to those totally inexperienced in the discipline.[41] Further, it is not surprising that after devoting a considerable amount of time to an experiment, that the subject should be unwilling to reveal that he was wasting his own time and that of the experimenter by taking part in a faulty experiment. It must not be assumed, however, that simply because subjects do not reveal their clandestine knowledge of the true purpose of an experiment that this necessarily biases the experimental results. Golding and Lichstenstein, for example, demonstrated that although their subjects were reluctant to reveal awareness of deception, they differed but little in their performance in the experiments compared to totally naive subjects.[42]

The lesson to be drawn is that more objective methods of detecting artifacts are necessary than simply asking the subject, in retrospect, the purpose of the experiment. Orne has argued that the problem of demand characteristics can be tackled by describing the procedure of the experiment to a separate group of subjects, similar in essential respects to the actual experimental subjects, and asking them to describe what the experiment is about. The ideal procedure would be to take these subjects through the actual experimental procedure with the actual apparatus used in the experiment (but without allowing them to make any actual response to the manipulations) and ask them to solve the problem of what the purpose of the experiment was. If the subjects report that they would behave in a certain manner and this corresponds to what the subjects actually do in the real experiment, then the hypothesis that the transparency of the experiment explains the experimental results becomes plausible. This, as Orne points out, does not prove the artifact explanation but simply increases confidence in it. The technique is one of approximation rather than proof.

The reason for this uncertainty is fairly clear. If we take, for example, an experiment in which a child is rewarded with a sweet every time he ties his shoe lace correctly and compare this with the results of an experiment in which the procedures are described to the subjects but they do not actually receive any rewards, one would not be too surprised to find that the results of the real experiment and the quasi-experiment correspond. This is partly because the process of reward is familiar and the consequences of the experimental method closely related to commonly observed processes. Little confidence would be placed on the demand characteristics explanation in these circumstances. On the other hand, where the relationship between the experimental methodology and commonly observed phenomena is not very close, there can be more certainty that the artifact explanation is more likely to be correct. Logically these methods cannot conclusively prove that the demand characteristics explanation is accurate, but one would prefer methodologies which cannot yield positive quasi-experiment results.

This idea of artifact in the Berkowitz type of experiment has been considered quite frequently by researchers in the field.[43] There is nothing intuitively obvious in the outcomes of these experiments (many people would feel that catharsis is as likely as an increase in aggression) and in many ways the experimental design is a little bit 'odd' to say the least. For example, is it not curious that an experimenter should anger and badger his subjects — surely the idea is for experimenters to be distant, affectively neutral, and to treat their subjects in as bland a fashion as possible? Isn't it a little strange that instead of showing us the boxer treating his friends meanly the experimenter has to read us an outline stressing this? Why is it so important if we are to be tested on our knowledge of the film content? Isn't it unexpected that supposedly liberal university researchers should be concerned with the effects of punishment on learning? What a coincidence it is that the subject should be allowed the opportunity to shock someone who offended them or to write a critical report to the Chairman of the psychology department! One would not wish to suggest that any of these factors are necessarily implicated in the experimental findings but only that they indicate a possibility which ought to be put to a test.

Berkowitz was questioned on this matter at a public meeting in 1966: Professor Isidor Chein of the New York University asked him 'Isn't it correct that college students are notoriously inclined to the expectations of the experiments so that they have a way of producing what the experimenter wants? Isn't it also true that when you say that physical acts of violence are involved, that it's a rather important qualifier in your statement, to wit, that they believe they are physically injuring somebody? Isn't it more correct to say that you believe that they believe?'[44]

Berkowitz's reply deserves attention. 'Our subjects, who are paid for participating in the research, get their rewards, and then go through some very intensive open-end interviews to determine to what extent these college students are concerned about giving us what we want. This is very standard practice. The subjects, by the way, are debriefed; that is, the experiment is explained to them afterwards. We are completely honest with them. We try to get them to be completely honest with us and we are quite convinced that these subjects, (1) do not suspect what it is that we want; and (2) are not attempting to act in order to please us or to put their best foot forward. That is all I can say. Obviously this isn't clinical, but it is our definite belief that the subjects are not play-acting'.

We have already seen some of the reasons for doubting the adequacy of post-experimental interviews as the basis for rejecting the artifact explanation. Page and Scheidt[45] have given us some further reasons to be suspicious of Berkowitz's assertions. This comes from an investigation of the demand characteristics of a study by Berkowitz and LePage[46] on the aggression eliciting effect of weapons. The study is not of the effect of vicarious aggression, although the experimental design was very similar, but with the presence of weapons replacing the violent filmed material. In a shock-machine type of study Berkowitz and LePage placed guns next to the shock button (suggesting that they had been left there by someone else) and found that these subjects were more extreme in their revenge for earlier electric shocks than subjects going through the same procedures but without guns being present. The assertion resulting from this being that weapons elicit aggression — 'the trigger pulls the finger'.

Page and Scheidt were rather suspicious about the outcome of this experiment partly because of its basic implausibility but also because the evidence against the demand characteristics view was weak (coming from post interviews). They decided that a replication of the original experiment was in order to check for certain possible artifacts. Following fairly precisely (but not exactly) Berkowitz and LePage's original methodology, certain aspects of the original results were found in this new experiment but the essential effect of the presence or absence of weapons was *not* replicated.

A second replication was attempted — this time increasing the match with the original study by using non-experimentally naive subjects and by emphasising the psychological distance between subject and 'stooge' (the possibility that the subject was shocking a friend might explain the first failure to replicate). Under these conditions it was found that the presence of weapons inhibited the level of shock given and that these sophisticated subjects gave fewer shocks when weapons were present ! Very detailed post-interviews revealed that many subjects were aware of what they were supposed to do in the experimental situation but that they, especially in the weapons present condition, leaned over backwards not to comply with this. This negativism is rather different to the compliance which might explain the results of the original experiment. This second failure to replicate is difficult to reconcile with Berkowitz's original findings, but Page and Scheidt supposed that it might be suspicion of deception which explained the negativism whereas demand awareness would explain the cooperation of the original experiment. The experiment was replicated for a third time but this time suspicion was reduced by making the stooge more plausible and credible. Demand awareness was increased by telling the subject not to worry about the guns, instead of trying to cover up by saying they belonged to a previous subject.

The results of this experiment both supported and disconfirmed those of the original study. It was found that naive subjects in the weapons present condition delivered less shocks than those in the weapons absent condition and that the very opposite applied to the more sophisticated subjects. Clearly these findings are best explained in terms of artifacts rather than in terms of 'true' experimental effects due to the presence of weapons in an aggressive situation. Certainly these findings should cause some concern about the validity of these aggression experiments and, by inference, about the validity of the effects of violent films in similar studies.

Howitt and Cumberbatch[47] chose to pursue the question of artifact in film-mediated violence experiments rather differently by using the non-experiment approach suggested by Orne. Further, instead of concentrating on the experimental designs which would most readily be seen as artificial, it was decided to consider those designs less obviously fraught with difficulty so that the most stringent test of the artifact hypothesis could be undertaken. For this reason experiments taking place in university psychology laboratories, using other than naive subjects, and using suspicious manipulations such as verbal qualifications explaining film content, were avoided. Since Hartmann's experiment described earlier was felt to be free of these difficulties and also to be well designed in other respects (using proper control groups, etc.) it was used in our study. Another advantage was that the complete script of the experimental procedure was available for this experiment, so replication would not be difficult.

The subjects in this experiment were 224 boys and girls in the sixteen to eighteen year age range. They were required to complete a questionnaire asking about the sort of levels and quantity of shock that they would give and what they thought the experimenter would want them to give in the circumstances of the experiment described to them in the questionnaire. In fact, there were six different questionnaires all told — one for each of the different conditions in Hartmann's experiment. Therefore, half of the questionnaires described the angering behaviour of the confederate and the other half described the more neutral treatment. A third of each of these described each of the three different film treatments.

If the experimental situation was completely free from demand characteristic pressures then it would be expected that the amount of shock given would not differ according to which experimental treatment the subject was responding to. Our data clearly showed that the treatments differed in the extent to which the subjects would deliver high electric shocks. This variation was due both to the film treatment and to the anger arousal procedure. Thus we suspect that artifacts in the methodology rather than true experimental effects may be producing the results of such experiments (the subjects just did not see the films which were supposed to have determined the results of the original experiment).

Although the results of the original experiment were not reproduced in total (not surprising in view of the radical differences between the circumstances of the two experiments) there was a high degree of correspondence. The own intentions measure was the most predictive (i.e. what the individual said he would do in the circumstances of the experiment) and the treatment means of the original and our experiment correlated highly and significantly. It is less certain whether the subject's perceptions of the experimenter's expectations form a satisfactory explanation. While there were differences in the cell means for the different treatments on this measure, the correlation between the level of shock predicted in our data and that given in the original experiment did not reach significance. However, experimenter expectations and demand characteristic explanations are quite distinct and, in sum, our data tends to support the latter explanation.

But it would be misleading to give the impression that this evidence finally and completely proves the inadequacy of these experiments. Researchers committed to the methodology employed by Berkowitz and others have investigated the possibility of these artifacts arising in their studies and have found evidence which they suggest excludes the artifact argument.

Berkowitz and Alioto[48] interviewed their subjects to investigate several dimensions of the problem. They asked them what they did in the experiment, what they thought the experimenter wanted them to do, and what they thought the other subject was supposed to do in the experiment (the confederate). The experimenter then rated the subjects according to their suspiciousness of the experiment. Interestingly enough there were many more suspicious subjects in the experimental film condition than in the control film condition. Why this should be without there being actual artifacts in methodology is unclear. Berkowitz and Alioto, however, make great play of the fact that those who were suspicious and rejected from the sample tend to deliver the least electric shocks:

The rejected men (who had been very aware of the deceptions and had grasped the connection between the film and the shocks given them) generally made the fewest attacks on the accomplice and, overall, tended to be more restrained than any other group of subjects. Instead of acting more violently, as the demand characteristics notion proposes, the more certain the subjects were that the study dealt with aggression, the less likely they were to shock the confederate.

All in all, the findings indicated that our significant condition differences arose in spite of the subjects' suspicions rather than because of them.

But, as we have already seen from the work of Page and Scheidt, the effects of experimental artifacts differ subtly according to rather minor differences in the nature of an experimental design, procedure, and subjects. For this reason it is not possible to accept Berkowitz and Alioto's argument as being definitive. What they do ably demonstrate is that artifacts may be expected in this situation. Furthermore, they fail to draw a line between suspiciousness and demand characteristics.

Goranson[49] argues from two studies that demand characteristics cannot explain the results of his experiments. In his first study he claims that the levels of suspiciousness of subjects was high but did not differ between experimental and control groups. Unfortunately the measure of suspicion he used was whether the subject thought that the confederate actually received the shocks sent. This tells us nothing of the suspicions about the experimental variables. However, in the second experiment several subjects suggested 'that the purpose might have been to study film effects on shock-giving'. No details other than this are provided. The data does not clearly tackle the artifacts issue and certainly does little to add confidence to the experimental methodology.

Finally Tannenbaum[50] explored the suspiciousness issue by using accomplices. Aware of the argument that the subject would be unlikely to divulge his 'guilty' secret to the experimenter in the post-interview situation, he designed a methodology which he hoped would overcome this. Instead of the post-experimental interview, the subject came to meet an accomplice of the experimenter who voiced suspicions about the experiment. This provided circumstances which might be conducive to the subject revealing his feelings about the experiment. No suspicions were forthcoming. It can be questioned whether one would expect that the subject would reveal his secrets in these circumstances. For one thing, it might be equally uncomfortable to reveal that one had 'behaved improperly' in the experiment to a stranger as it would be to the experimenter.

Clearly, the evidence for and against the artifact explanation is contradictory. However, one point must be made. Those researchers who are 'against' the artifact explanation seem to expect that the subject will be completely coherent and aware of the details of the experimental hypothesis. This is probably not the case. It is more likely that the ideas are only half-formed in the subject's mind and not capable of full articulation. In this case the more subtle rating methodologies or the behavioural methodology of Page and Scheidt would seem to have a better chance of detecting artifacts. From the data, this indeed seems to be the case.

Final evaluation of the artifact explanation of these studies must be left in abeyance until a broad range of studies are available to guide this assessment. At this stage, it would seem that the artifact hypothesis remains feasible although there is a certain amount of evidence on both sides. However, the limitations of these experiments are not ultimately revolved around the internal validity of the method but their relationship to real world processes. The artifact explanations might well explain the inconsistency in the studies but, in the end, this is not the crucial point.

A FURTHER ALTERNATIVE: DOES AROUSAL CAUSE EXPERIMENTAL EFFECTS?

There is another reason, perhaps conceptually a little more complicated, for doubting the relevance of the Berkowitz type of experiment to the applied question of the effects of mass media violence. This comes largely from the research of Percy Tannenbaum,[51] but there are clues earlier in the history of the topic pointing in essentially the same sort of direction.[52] The argument is that it is not specifically the effect of aggression arousal which determines response to aggressive films but simply the level of physiological arousal. To put it simply, aggressive film has its effects because it produces generalised physiological arousal (almost a heightened state of activity) which increases the probability and intensity of any response that the individual is required to perform. Thus it is not just aggression that might be expected to increase after a film, but also response to humour, cooperative behaviour, and so forth. Again, the aggressive film is not the only sort of film to increase aggressive behaviour, and an erotic or exhilarating comedy film would be just as effective in eliciting aggression. Clearly, to the extent that this theory is adequate it diminishes proportionally any credence we could give to the Berkowitz experiments as having implications for the control of media content. One could scarcely believe that political decisions could be made to stop excitement from reaching our television or cinema screens!

Walters and Brown[53] provided the first support of the view that any sort of high magnitude behaviour (high intensity, high activity) increases the likelihood of aggressive behaviour in laboratory conditions. They showed that children trained to high activity levels on a lever pressing task also tended to be more aggressive in an interpersonal setting compared with children trained to low activity behaviour on the same non-aggressive task. Geen and O'Neall[54] replicated the essence of Berkowitz's experiments but instead of using the angering/non-angering manipulation they subjected their subjects to either high or low levels of white noise to arouse them to high and low levels of physiological arousal. It was found that Berkowitz's results were essentially replicated despite the fact that the subjects were not angered but simply aroused. This study alone would make us somewhat suspicious of Berkowitz's theory and others employing much the same methodology.

The studies of Tannenbaum simply extend our confusion to its limits. Tannenbaum and his students have carried out a large number of studies in this area and, amongst other things, have found:

1. That a physiologically arousing but non-aggressive erotic film produces more shocking in the usual experimental set-up than an aggressive but less physiologically arousing film.
2. That a humorous film is effective in arousing aggression compared to control films.
3. That humorous and aggressive films tend to be equally effective in increasing humorous response to humorous material.
4. That in conditions where the subject has to reward the 'learner' rather than punish him, erotic films increase rewarding behaviour.

These findings give considerable support for the view that emotional arousal is effective in replicating the results of the Berkowitz style experiments although there remain a number of difficulties. For example, it has been shown by Berkowitz in his later experiments that when a highly arousing control film is used (a track racing film) the effects of the experimental film are still demonstrable. Perhaps a demand characteristics explanation could account for some of the effects which arousal differences in aggressive and control films cannot. Even so, the theory yields some interesting speculations. For example, the researchers monitored viewers' responses to some of the films used in the early studies of the effect of vicarious violence. They compared the arousal potential of the experimental film *(Champion)* of Berkowitz's studies with that of Feshbach's early study *(Body and Soul)* and found that arousal decreased at the end of the Feshbach film. Tannenbaum has written:

> Thus, a possible alternative interpretation of Feshbach's findings is suggested. Instead of postulating a symbolic catharsis formulation, one could argue that a build-up of excitation followed by a marked reduction would lead to a lessening of aggressive behaviour. [55]

Whatever the final conclusions of Tannenbaum's research — and it should be noted that he does not interpret them in terms relevant to the public debate — there seems to be absolutely no justification for regarding the Berkowitz type of study as being relevant to policy decisions. Certainly we need to look elsewhere for proof of the assertion that media violence causes violence in society.

Zillman and Johnson[56] have added a further dimension to this. They argued the point that the original studies of the Berkowitz type have failed to control for an important factor — that of the effects of being shown no film at all. They added to the basic electric shock paradigm a no exposure condition, while other groups watched a highly violent clip from *The Wild Bunch* or a neutral film *(Marco Polo's*

Travels). They wanted to know whether it was possible that the neutral films in the Berkowitz type experiment were depressing the aggressive behaviour of the viewer, rather than the aggressive films increasing aggression. Their evidence indeed showed that this was the case. Although the neutral film depressed the level of aggression in the audience, there were no differences between exposure to a violent film and the effects of seeing no film in terms of the willingness of the subjects to deliver electric shocks! Physiological measures indicated that the neutral film depressed arousal processes, whereas these remained constant for the no film and aggressive film conditions.

The policy decision implied by Zillman and Johnson's research, as well as that of Tannenbaum, would suggest that in order to reduce the level of violence in society the television audience should be bored silly (perhaps by showing them *Marco Polo's Travels* thrice daily). Certainly there would be no point in simply removing violent programmes from television since this should not affect the level of violence in society. Obviously, we are not offering these suggestions as serious possibilities but as illustrations of the ludicrous and impracticable contortions to which such laboratory studies will lead us.

CONCLUSIONS

It would be fair to say that the results of experimental studies of the effects of vicarious aggression are not so straightforward as researchers have suggested. The catharsis studies, despite the theoretical problem of whether aggression can be purged by witnessing vicarious aggression, suggest that films can have an inhibitory influence even if this is mediated through processes of the arousal of aggression anxiety. For this reason alone it would be inaccurate to suggest that vicarious aggression necessarily has the stimulating effect attributed to it. When the laboratory experiments are compared with the field experiments the need for caution is emphasised. As far as can be judged, the results of the field experiments suggest the inadequacy of the generalisations from the laboratory studies. Since it is well known that effects found in the laboratory are often diluted in real life situations, this difference comes as no surprise. Laboratory studies typically try to detect the unconfounded effect of a stimulus free from the complications of the real world, whereas the field experiments try to evaluate how the results of the laboratory fare in the harsh and critical test-bed of everyday behaviour. The studies of physiological arousal further reduce our confidence in the relevance of this research.

Chapter Five is concerned with the correlational studies linking mass media exposure with aggression and delinquency and further extends our treatment of laboratory-field relationships in the area of the effects of vicarious aggression. However, because of the difficulties of cause and effect relationship in such studies, they are best considered in conjunction with the experimental approaches in this chapter. The next chapter tries to evaluate the adequacy of these studies by emphasising the intervening processes which might explain the effects of exposure to vicarious aggression and actual overt aggression in the viewer. This concentration on processes can be seen as part of the means of validating the conclusions of the laboratory experiments.

CHAPTER FOUR
MECHANISMS OF MEDIA EFFECT

While the previous chapter casts doubt on the relevance of many of the experimental studies of vicarious violence to the debate about the effects of mass media violence, this in itself is not sufficient proof that the media do not affect the level of violence in society. Most are essentially irrelevant. We have seen that good experimental field studies tend to yield no evidence that television violence causes the viewer to be aggressive — but there is so little available evidence here that caution must be exercised. The laboratory experiments cause the no-effects thesis little worry. In this chapter we consider the mechanisms and processes by which it has been asserted that the mass media influence the aggressiveness of the audience. In many ways the mechanisms of media effect on the audience are essential stepping-stones in our understanding of the mass communications process. If it is consistently found that the processes thought to bridge the gap between the content of the mass media and the effects of the mass media are unsupported by empirical research, one must begin to question whether such effects are likely. If, to take a parallel, we were able to show under laboratory conditions that the hare invariably runs faster than the turtle, we would certainly have reason to doubt that the turtle won the race by fleetfootedness.

Such considerations are a step removed from the question of the effects of mass media violence but, in the absence of satisfactory direct evidence, the validation of such intermediary processes gains importance. Our reading of the evidence on intermediary processes between exposure and effect is that little faith can be put in identification, imitation, desensitisation, attitude change, and 'triggering' as mediating between mass media violence and violence in society. This is, of course, to be expected if the media have no effect on the level of violence in society, but more difficult to reconcile with the 'media cause violence' claim. Although there has been some evidence, collected in isolation, for and against a variety of these postulated processes, it has apparently not been considered that the systematic review of evidence concerning intermediary mechanisms is an essential step in understanding the relationship between the mass media and the audience. Perhaps this is not surprising in a climate of assumed effect of the mass media (whether in the direction of increasing societal violence or decreasing it) but one cannot help but think that this reluctance has impeded the progress of social science in reaching a satisfactory conclusion to the whole question of the effects of mass media violence.

As we will see, many of the mechanisms of media effect have entered what might be called popular scientific folklore. Frequently they have been considered to be operative even in the absence of reliable scientific evidence. Often the concepts have been used interchangeably without formal differentiation but, as we are in a difficult area in which social scientists cannot agree, one can scarcely blame the layman for such confusions. It is probably worthwhile trying to indicate something of what we mean by identification, imitation, desensitisation, and so forth; and while we cannot define precisely the meaning of most of the terms, we can at least ease the readers' difficulties when faced with the technicalities of the research data.

Despite the fact that in much of the literature on the subject the concept of identification is regarded as stemming from Freudian psycho-analytic theory, the consideration of Freudian theory is for the most part a fruitless effort in respect of the effects of the mass media. For one thing, the theory is mainly concerned with the process of personal development in relation to the omnipotent parent from the early stages of infancy, which seems to have little bearing on the mass media, for such mundane reasons as television is scarcely an activity of the cradle, even in this day and age (this is also to ignore the more elaborate psychological objections to the theory).[1] Some writers[2] have seized upon the Freudian notion 'identification with the aggressor' as being relevant to the question of the effects of mass media violence. At first sight the idea seems reasonable, but in Freudian theory identification with the aggressor refers to a defence mechanism where a person who is threatened by a powerful figure reduces this threat by acting like the object of his fear. Thus little children may pretend to be daddy to invest themselves with fearsome qualities which will match those of daddy whom they fear. The essential objection to the relevance of this process in the context of the mass media is that personal and direct threat of persons in the real world is not to be found in the media. The essential psychodynamic relationship seen by Freud is lacking.

The major difficulty with the concept of identification, to put it crudely, is that you don't know that it's happening until it's happened. Thus, in the classical sense, it is not known whether the child has identified with the mother until he displays some behaviour which matches that of the mother. For this reason certain social psychologists have rejected this and similar concepts and substituted the more generic term of imitation or modelling to cover all such contingencies.[3] This is sensible as both imitation and identification resemble each other when we consider their behavioural manifestations alone. However, others, implicitly if rarely explicitly, have tended to define identification in terms of a predispositional affect for a mass media character.[4] This would imply that if a child has a positive feeling for a character (for example, he might like the way the character dresses or the character might remind him of a cherished friend) this generalises to a liking for other aspects of the character — possibly as far as the character's aggressiveness. The child might like the way Trampas in *The Virginian* treats women kindly, and thus become more accepting of his aggressiveness. This sort of definition or identification might be termed an 'affective disposition' towards acceptance of the total personality of the media character. There is any amount of evidence from the social psychological literature to suggest that such strains towards a consistent evaluation of others are common.[5] Assuming this, the question remains whether for aggression, which is subject to drastic and powerful socialising pressures, such processes would be powerful enough to have much effect, if any at all.

Imitation is rather simpler to define — it merely involves a one-to-one correspondence between the behaviour of a mass media character and the behaviour of the young viewer. Nevertheless, just because there is a correspondence between what a character does on the screen and what a child does in real life, it is not proper to assume that the actions of the screen character *caused* the child's behaviour. It is important to bear in mind that many of the things which occur on the screen are likely to occur in real life in any event. Thus baseline measurements of the frequency of such events in real life are necessary before one can adequately describe the effects of the mass media on imitative behaviour. Consider also that the conditions and context of a real life event are often very different from those portrayed on the screen. Small boys in short pants playing cowboys and Indians in the school playground just do not look like the Indians riding down the mountainside in the Western film. Obviously if imitation does occur in real life as a consequence of the child watching a particular character (or model as the jargon would have it), it is partly a generalisation from the original behaviour portrayed by the character and the original context. It would be expected, then, that imitative learning should generalise away from the situation in which the behaviour was initially portrayed.[6]

The idea that the media should have their effects through the process of attitude change is very persuasive, at least at a superficial level. For one thing it is almost a truism to suggest that people's behaviour is mediated through complex cognitive processes in which fairly rational responses are made to complicated material. For another, there is a quantity of social psychological and sociological literature to show that the mass media, at least in fairly limited instances, can have a profound effect on the attitudes and opinions of individuals.[7]

Obviously it may well be the case that attitudes to aggression are not amenable to the influence of the mass media, but it is questionable whether a change in attitude necessarily implies a corresponding change in behaviour. We will deal with these points more fully when we discuss the relevant data.

If one were to be flippant it would not be very far from the truth to suggest that the idea that the media might 'trigger' unbalanced minds into bizarre action is a last-ditch effort to hold on to the idea that the mass media may have some effect on violence in society. Certainly, it has some intuitive appeal and one survey has shown that of all the possible effects of mass media violence, the public are most likely to believe that television violence triggers violent acts from people who are maladjusted or mentally unstable.[8] Isolated and individual cases such as Brady and the Moors murders which implicated sadistic fiction, and many reported cases in which aggressive or criminal individuals have excused themselves with claims like 'television gave me the idea' and 'the cinema dun it, guv' may be the basis for this concern.[9] Since such cases have little or no scientific worth they need to be ignored for the purpose of forming conclusions about the effects of mass media violence. Unfortunately they consist of the vast bulk of our evidence in favour of the triggering effect of the mass media on unstable minds. The one study which is relevant, and scientifically more acceptable, considers the effects of vicarious experience on the behaviour of normal and 'emotionally disturbed' children. This will be discussed later.

The effect of the media on our sensitivity to violence is the final mechanism for which we will present relevant research findings. Briefly the desensitisation hypothesis argues that repeated portrayals of violence in the mass media blunts our emotional response to such material gradually over time and we end up being unable to respond appropriately. There are many problems which make evaluation of this desensitisation idea difficult, the major one being knowing just what it is meant to imply. As will be seen, it is established psychological knowledge that emotional response to any stimulus will become weaker and weaker after repeated presentation of that stimulus. However, this effect of habituation is not necessarily such a bad thing and its implications are not so far reaching as one would at first assume. For example, it is fortunate that ambulance drivers learn to overcome their emotional responses to motorway accidents which would leave the rest of us quivering and impotent. Obviously it is not the blunting of the emotional, physiological response *per se* which is the problem but whether it reduces concomitantly our compassion, our desire to help victims of attack, our inhibitions against injuring others, and our moral outrage at such events. To introduce such considerations is, of course, to impinge on the effects of the media on attitudes to aggression and some of the other processes we have described.

Having outlined some of the major concerns about the processes of mass media effect, we are in a better position to evaluate the evidence bearing on the various mechanisms. It should be emphasised at the outset that most of the data deal specifically with the involvement of these mechanisms in violence and that they may well not apply in other areas such as health programmes and others dealing with poorly socialised areas of experience. A few examples of this will be given in the text but the important thing to remember is that our primary concern is with the question of violence and we would not wish to generalise further than this on the basis of the vast bulk of the data to hand.

IDENTIFICATION

In the code of standards published by the British Broadcasting Corporation[10] to guide producers, particularly of children's programmes, a major point is that bad habits in 'good' characters (such as chain-smoking, hitting below the belt) are to be avoided. This is tantamount to saying that the child will be influenced by the hero (a character for which the child will probably have a strong positive feeling) to adopt or see in a more favourable light the 'bad' behaviours of that hero. Thus the concept of dispositional identification is enshrined in the formal documents of broadcasting institutions. The British Broadcasting Corporation is not alone in its concern — Schramm, Lyle and Parker have stated it as a 'fact':

> There is no doubt that the child can more easily store up behaviours and beliefs which he has imaginatively shared with the character with whom he identifies.[11]

This statement is based on a study of recall of film content by children identifying with film characters and does not mean that this learning is in fact put into operation.[12] André Glucksmann seemed to be the sole voice questioning the central position given to identification when he suggested that it has not been proved that all the hero's activities tend to be 'carried out' by the young viewer. He also offered the opinion that it is possible that imitative identification with the star remains limited to secondary aspects of behaviour related to fashion (clothing, superficial relations between the sexes).[13]

Glucksmann's reservations are, of course, critical since mass media personalities and heroes are tremendously important to many members of the audience. One has only to consider the fan clubs, the magazines devoted to media personalities, the use of media characters in merchandising and the amount of money devoted to these things, to be convinced of the central role of the media in the lives of people.[14] However, it is a giant step from noting that these phenomena are common to believing that aggression in society is affected adversely by them. It would also be wrong to assume that mass media characters are the most popular identification figures. Howitt and Cumberbatch asked 11 — 15 year olds to indicate how much they would like to be like certain mass media characters, friends, and their mother and father. The data showed that the children's parents were the most popular choices. It would seem reasonable to interpret this as implying that identification with parents at home could be a more powerful determinant of their behaviour than any mass media character or personality. It might also be pointed out that the children's own class teacher was very poorly represented in comparison to some mass media personalities and characters.

The purely experimental evidence concerning the effects of identification on the child is limited in quantity. Howitt and Cumberbatch[16] presented evidence to suggest that identification with a character had no effect on children's attitudes concerning the aggressive behaviour of that character. The children were shown a lengthy excerpt from the film *Chick's Day* (which is about a street-corner boy's adventures) in order that the children could form some sort of affective feeling for this character — whether it be liking or loathing. The children were then asked to fill in rating scales designed to measure their degree of affect for this character and a composite 'identification' score calculated on the basis of such questions as 'How much do you like Chick?', 'How much would you like Chick as a brother?', and 'How much would you like Chick as a friend?' This was then used to divide the subjects into two groups — one group consisting of individuals high on identification with Chick, the other group consisting of those individuals who did not have such a strong positive feeling for him. The next important step in the experiment was to measure whether the children high on identification with Chick would be more willing than the other group to accept Chick's violent behaviour. Since it was possible that the children formed their initial judgements of Chick partly on the basis of his aggressive behaviour during the excerpt that we showed them, it was necessary to incorporate a control group for which the aggressive behaviour was attributed to another character. In order to do this we prepared two alternative versions of a second questionnaire. In one case a violent act was attributed to Chick and in the other case it was attributed to a character called John Davies who had not been in the excerpt shown. The violent act was described as follows: 'Later, in town, John Davies (who was not in the excerpt shown you) is quietly minding his own business when he sees a local drunk acting insultingly towards a young woman, who is obviously frightened and upset. John Davies approaches the drunk, pushes him away from the woman and, losing his temper, punches him in the stomach. The drunk tries to run away but John Davies grabs him and knocks his unconscious with many blows.' The version attributing the act to Chick was identical except in so far as the phrase 'John Davies (who was not in the excerpt shown you)' and all references to John Davies were replaced by the name Chick. We then asked the children to say how bad they thought that the aggressive act was, whether the drunk should have been beaten as much as he was, whether the character had meant to hurt the man as much as he did and other items designed to discover the children's evaluations of the violent act.

The results of this experiment clearly show that identification with the mass media hero had absolutely no effect on evaluation of the violent act. To make doubly sure of the adequacy of this conclusion we repeated the experiment in all essential details except that we used an excerpt from the film *Billy Budd*. This allowed us to check whether the fact that Chick fell more into the category of 'baddy' than the category hero had any bearing on our conclusions. However, the results were to all intents and purposes exactly the same, and such differences as there were between the two studies explicable on the basis of chance. We then decided that it was possible that our essentially negative results might be due to the relatively short amount of time during which the child had to form affective feelings for the character and so we repeated the experiment twice but using an established media figure — Trampas from the Western series *The Virginian* — as the central character in our little story.[18] Since this character was familiar to most children — the series having run for several years in Great Britain — the fact that our data again showed that mass media identification had no effect on aggressive attitudes means that the earlier finding could not be attributed to the short exposure of our subjects to the film excerpts in the earlier studies. The conclusion that identification plays no part in the evaluation of aggressive acts is warranted.

On searching through the correlational research on this question we were able to muster a considerable amount of evidence from field and similar studies which supported our conclusion — not just at the attitudinal level but also at the behavioural level. Grant Noble compared the identifications of delinquent and a matched sample of non-delinquent boys for television heroes, fathers, and best friends.[19] The central hypothesis that delinquents more often than the controls would over-identify with television heroes was not substantiated, in accordance with our findings. That is, there was no evidence to suggest that the delinquent boys perceived themselves more like television heroes than did the control subjects, and it was equally true that the delinquent boys did not wish to be like television heroes to any greater degree than did the matched control group. On the other hand, there was evidence to suggest that delinquent boys, more often than controls, perceived themselves to be less like their best friends and their father. Noble suggests that for delinquents the television hero is a much more salient identification figure than he is for the control group, since friends and fathers did not emerge as powerful identification figures for delinquents. That is, he argues that because delinquents and controls did not differ in their attachment for television heroes, while delinquents identified less closely with the real life individuals, the television hero is a more important identification figure for delinquents than for more normal boys. This is, of course, a weak assertion in that it is possible to argue from the same data that fathers and best friends are figures for negative identification and these are more likely to be rejected or used as negative models for behaviour by the delinquents. An interesting finding which might be mentioned in passing is that the delinquents identified with pro-social aggressive heroes more closely than with the baddies.

Halloran, Brown and Chaney also found no evidence to suggest that delinquents (probationers) identified with or preferred aggressive heroes and heroines any more than a matched control sample, although there was some evidence to suggest that probationers rather liked figures from the world of popular music.[20] McLeod, Atkin and Chaffee[21] found only one significant correlation of aggressive attitudes with identification with aggressive heroes controlling for sex and school placement. Milgram and Shotland[22] found no relation of identification with imitating anti-social (but not aggressive) behaviours. However, Turner and Berkowitz[23] found (using Berkowitz's usual experimental method) that individuals told by the experimenter to identify with the aggressive character tended to deliver the greatest electric shocks. It should be realised that this procedure is as artificial as any of the others used by the Wisconsin researchers.

Howitt and Cumberbatch carried out a study of the effects of identification on imitation of mass media characters.[24] Essentially what they did was to ask school children to name those children in their class who copied aggressive television characters. It was found that those children nominated by their peers as being imitators of the mass media (even allowing for possible artifacts such as sex and popularity) did not differ from their classmates in their liking for aggressive television characters.

Clearly the evidence (with the exception of the study by Turner and Berkowitz) is unanimously against the notion that television personalities and characters dispose children to aggression. The studies of attitudes, delinquency, and imitation all point to the same conclusion. There is even evidence that aggressive boys are no more likely to identify with comic-book aggressive heroes than are normal or even excessively socialised children (those who have learned the 'proper' ways of behaviour too well).[25] In this particular study by Karp, one of the tasks the boys performed was to read two comic-book stories. In one case the leading characters were gangsters and in the other case the leading characters were law officials. In *The Wrong Road* three gangsters, Johnny Boland, his brother Bart Boland, and Eddy

Sherman, stage a jail-break, a hold-up, invade a home at gun-point, hide out at a girl friend's house, and eventually meet their well-deserved end — death and capture by the police. In the other story, *How to Get a Killer*, 'the hero, Mike Devlin, is an ingenious, resourceful and courageous special agent who strives to get evidence against a vicious racketeer and murderer. Without firing a shot, this top-notch operator, with his tricky techniques, succeeds in his mission.' Obviously these various comic book stories cover a wide range of 'hero' and might be expected to differentiate aggressive children from the others. Karp's measure of identification was to ask the boy, after he had read the comic, the question 'Suppose we were going to make a play of this comic and you had first choice to play any part you wanted to play, which would you choose?' Unexpectedly, on the grounds of the assumptions about the effects of mass media characters, but fully in accordance with the evidence presented above, there were absolutely no differences between the three groups in terms of their identification. Obviously, this finding is incompatible with the worries expressed about the effects of the mass media.

On the other hand, outside the literature on violence a certain amount of evidence suggests that the audience's emotive reactions to a communicator can affect the willingness of the audience to accept his message. For example, those stongly prejudiced against Negroes are less likely to change their attitude if the communicator is coloured- than if he is white.[26] This disparity between our argument and the evidence from the field of attitude change is in all probability due to the fact that we were studying a topic of some importance to the lives of our respondents — aggression — whereas the other studies were concerned with more trivial themes such as attitude to mathematics. Additionally, there is a study by Bandura and Huston using real life models which suggests that the affect the child had for the model can influence the child's behaviour.[27] In this study the model either behaved in a warm, nurturant manner towards the child or was distant and cold. It was found that the nurturant model was copied by the child more than was the cold model. Obviously the face-to-face situation employed in this study differs markedly from that of the mass media child relationship — for one thing the nurturant model in real life could withdraw her affection if the child did not 'reward her' by adopting her behaviours. Such a state of balance is impossible between the child and his mass media hero. Interestingly enough, although this study involved a measure of imitation of aggression, there was *no* tendency for the different sorts of model to produce significantly different levels of aggressive imitation. The playful aggressive behaviour used in this study was attractive to all children no matter what their relationship to the model. This finding was apparently unexpected by the researchers and preceded a later series of experiments designed to investigate the imitation of aggression in more detail. This later research has become important in the debate on mass media violence but will be discussed in more detail shortly when the issue of imitation is examined more closely. Suffice to say that the measures taken of aggression are not considered to be of anything other than playful aggression. Because the studies conflicting with our own argument deal with relatively unimportant and weakly socialised aspects of life, it is suggested that they have little bearing on the question of the effects of identification with aggressive media characters since there is much more salient data available.

All of this is not to say that the concept of identification is not of some importance and that researchers should not pay the topic considerable attention. What would be wrong, on the other hand, would be to argue that identification is a major agent in the socialisation of highly sanctioned behaviours. One would not wish to deny on the basis of the available evidence that the child who identified with a pop singer might be influenced by this to buy similar clothes to those of his idol or to buy music magazines featuring him, but it would be a mistake to attach undue importance to this as an agent of social learning. Identification with media characters, it has been shown in recent research, is not as common as might be supposed and depends on such factors as age, sex, and social position.[28] The researcher who could tell us why children form such links with such distant individuals would no doubt be contributing greatly to our understanding of children and the mass media, but he would be doing us a disservice if he emphasised the unproven and, perhaps, disproven adverse effects of such feelings on children's aggressive behaviour.

IMITATION

There is a close correspondence between the concepts of identification and imitation — not that they are identical but simply that they boil down to very much the same thing. An essential difference between the two is that the concept of identification implies some sort of emotional tie between the model and child, whereas imitation refers to the matching of the child's behaviour to that of the model whether or not this be mediated through the process of identification with the model.

It is quite easy to express in a nutshell the present state of our knowledge about imitation. Few would deny that imitation from the mass media is a possibility, the problem is whether in actual fact it occurs. This is a simple point and it is probably difficult for the outsider to understand why the distinction is not maintained by researchers in the field. The reasons for this are partly historic and partly embedded in past conceptions of the nature of human learning. The typical theory of learning put forward by psychologists during the first half of the century had the central tenet that learning proceeds little by little by a process of building up from the simple to the complex. It was rarely considered feasible that learning could be complete in a single 'trial'. Repetition and the addition of small elements of the whole were the cornerstones of early conceptions of human learning. The methods of learning multiplication tables by rote and repetition employed on many of us at school are not very far from completely illustrating the application of these theories. However, as everyone knows, in many circumstances it is far more efficacious merely to copy other individuals rather than to go through the process of building from small elements of the complex whole. Psychologists, unfortunately, had not bothered to observe their own behaviour since they were too busy teaching rats to pull levers. It was against this sort of perspective on human learning that Bandura and his colleagues at Stanford University began their classic studies of imitation.[29] As research on the psychology of human learning and child development we have absolutely no objection to the work of Bandura and his colleagues. We are rather less enthusiastic about the relevance of their research to the question of the effects of violence in the mass media. Perhaps a description of Bandura's style of research would help the reader at this point. We will return to the objections later.

Bandura's[30] subjects have been children of roughly pre-school age — an important consideration in view of the nature of the design. The essential features of the design were the exposure of the subject to a model who behaves aggressively, the frustration of the subject, and the final observation of the extent to which the children adopted the model's aggressive behaviour. More specifically, the child was met by an experimenter who took him into a room and sat him down either to watch a film projected onto a screen, a film presented by a means of a television console in such a way as to encourage the child to think it was a real television programme, or a live model in the same room in the laboratory. The sex of the model varied as did the format of the films. In one condition the model was simply the same as the real life model but filmed; in another condition — the cartoon condition — the model was presented as a cartoon cat with cartoon or Disney-like backgrounds. The content of the films in other respects was standard and identical to the real life model's behaviour. It consisted of the model beating a large inflatable plastic clown (called a Bobo or a Bozo doll) in a highly distinctive manner while calling out unusual slogans to emphasise the uniqueness of the model's behaviour (such as 'Whack him, eh'). Following this the children were frustrated by showing them some attractive toys which they were then informed they could not play with. Finally, the children were led into a room containing very similar objects to the ones the model had used and were ostensibly left alone to play. In reality they were being observed through special

73

one-way mirrors. The dependent variable was the amount of aggressive behaviour imitated. Several categories of behaviour were measured including straightforward imitation and non-imitative aggressive. One control group did not witness the model's aggressive behaviour either on film or in real life, and so was only subjected to the dependent measures and the associated frustration. The other control group witnessed the model playing constructively, were frustrated and then exposed to the measurement situation. These controls were designed to give baselines on which to judge the extent that aggressive imitation could be explained away by chance. They also made allowance for the fact that exposure to a model, whether aggressive or not, might have some influence on the aggressive behaviour of the child.

It was found that the children exposed to the aggressive models imitated the model to a greater degree than could be expected by chance, since the level of 'imitative' behaviour in the control groups was significantly lower than that of the experimental groups. Contrary to our expectations there was no tendency for the real life model to be more effective in eliciting aggressive imitation than the filmed models and, if anything, the cartoon model was the most effective moulder of behaviour. This study was followed by a whole series of others which, for example, investigated the effects of the model being rewarded for his behaviour on imitation.[31] But, rather than extending the basic paradigm, it is important that we explore the relevance of this one study to the question of the effects of mass media violence. Our criticisms apply equally to the later research. Bandura has drawn stronger conclusions from this study than many other social scientists would be willing to:

> The finding that film-mediated models are as effective as real-life models in eliciting and transmitting aggressive responses indicates that televised models may serve as important sources of behaviour and can no longer be ignored in conceptualisations of personality development. Indeed, most youngsters probably have more exposure to prestigeful televised male models than to their own fathers. With further advances in mass media and audiovisual technology, pictorially presented models, mainly through television, are likely to play an increasingly influential role in shaping personality patterns, and in modifying attitudes and social norms.[32]

This statement consists of essentially two elements;

1. That it has been shown that film-mediated models are directly comparable with real-life models as sources for children's behavioural repertoire.
2. That these findings apply to the real world outside of the laboratory situation.

Many writers have argued that this jump from the laboratory to the real world is far too big to swallow. The points against Bandura's argument are many and some were summarised in essence by Hartley: She wrote:

First, it (Bandura's study) suggests that behavior towards inanimate objects like toys, is equated with social behavior, a suggestion which is not generally supported in the literature. In fact, the bulk of the literature supports an opposite view that children will express toward inanimate objects feelings they would not dare to show openly toward other persons . . . Other differences between the laboratory situations of the studies . . . and real-life viewing situations can be summarized as follows: the presence of several possible identification figures in ordinary entertainment displays versus a solitary identification figure in the laboratory material; feedback in the form of consequence of behavior in ordinary televised situations versus no consequences to the 'aggressor' in the experimental film; reinforcement of some kind from parents and others in real life versus no response to post-viewing behaviour in the experiment; unlikeliness of the occurence of an exact reproduction of the filmed stimulus situation in real life versus the painstaking provision of exactly similar toys in the laboratory; the relative simplicity of the series of acts in the experimental film versus the greater complexity of sequence usually present in television films; the repetition of exactly the same acts in more usual sequence of film displayed; the concentration of aggressive behavior without the more usual dilution with non-aggressive behaviour.[33]

Some reviewers have suggested that Hartley's critical review may have been unobjective because it was financed by the Columbia Broadcasting System. Nevertheless it is difficult to reject the very valid criticisms which Hartley makes.[34] Take for example the argument that attacking the Bobo clown is not valid as an indicator or real life aggression. In fact, in the original report of the experiment, there is evidence to suggest that this may well be the case. Part of the selection procedure for inclusion of children in the experimental and control groups was equating them in terms of teacher-ratings of their aggressiveness. One would expect that the children who the teachers said were aggressive would actually attack the plastic clown far more readily than the non-aggressive children if aggression against the Bobo clown is adequate as a predictor of real life aggression. That this was *not* the case is evidence against the view that the findings are generalisable to real life. The question of whether such imitative actions have any bearing on the effects of the media may be questioned along lines other than the validity of the doll as a measure of aggression. As Hartley implies, there is a considerable difference between behaviour modelled on television and the real life settings in which children exist. Recent research following the kind of design adopted by Bandura has shown that if the 'aggressive play' situation is less similar to that shown in the film, the amount of imitative aggression shown by children is drastically reduced. Additionally, the play situation provided by Bandura involves exposing children to fairly novel kinds of toys. Other research has demonstrated that if children are allowed some pre-experience of Bozo dolls then the amount of imitative aggression shown may also be reduced. This is essentially the same point as can be made about the effects of television on attitudes. Television is more likely to show some effect on its audience in areas which are completely outside their normal behaviour and experience. When it comes to the 'crunch' television is ineffective.

Given the unusual nature of the stimulus used in Bandura's experiments (the Bozo doll), perhaps the greater cause for concern arises from whether or not the imitative 'aggression' of Bandura's experiments generalise to aggression of a non-imitative kind. After all, for the experiments to have any relevance to real life the effects would have to be robust enough to extend far beyond the one-to-one relationship between the stimulus and response situations of the modelling experiments. There is little or no evidence from the original studies to suggest that non-imitative aggression following exposure to the models in Bandura's studies is significantly higher than in the control groups. Bandura has argued that these measures of non-imitative aggression are not really valid as measures of the effect of modelling on non-imitative aggression.[35] His reason is straightforward: because there is only a limited amount of time available in which aggression can take place, if the child exhibits a high level of imitative aggression there is little time available in which he can manifest signs of non-imitative aggression. If one was to spend all day washing the car there would be no opportunity to wash the dishes! In many ways this argument is persuasive and Bandura feels that the best way of exploring the effects of modelling on non-imitative aggression is procedures such as those of Berkowitz which are described in the previous chapter and which we claim to be fraught with difficulties of their own. Howitt[36] has suggested a formula by which the amount of time devoted to non-imitative aggression can be corrected to make allowance for the level of imitative aggression manifested by the child. This consists simply of standardising the non-imitative aggression scores of each child so that for each child they are considered against a standard amount of time available for non-imitative aggression. Even when this was done the essential conclusion remains the same — aggressive modelling has no effect on non-imitative aggression!

Field studies of imitative behaviour are rarities because of the problems in deciding what actually comprises imitation. Howitt and Cumberbatch have provided one of the exceptions to this principle.[37] Although their study yielded some interesting findings, there was no basis in their data for implying that the mass media cause violence in society. They found that the children who are rated as copying from the mass media aggressive hero are somewhat different from those who are rated low on copying. For one thing they are more popular (Howitt and Cumberbatch showed that their ratings as being copiers are not the consequence of the popular child being nominated simply because his was the first name which came to the mind of the raters) and for another they tend to be first-born and only children more frequently than those rated low on copying from the mass media. It seems possible that television programmes are utilised by certain children on the basis of their instrumental value in achieving popularity. Further evidence for this comes from the fact that the more popular children in our sample said more frequently that they copied things from the popular music programme *Top of the Pops* than did the less popular children.

The evidence concerning the mass media and imitation provides us with little convincing proof that the level of violence in society can be adversely influenced by the direct imitation of mass media models. It is not denied that imitation can shape human behaviour, but the evidence for its influence on aggressive behaviour is certainly very weak. Besides the arguments put forward above, we must bear in mind the whole question of the motivations for adopting these behaviours. Although it is easy to see that the children in Bandura's experiments would be keen to play with the Bobo clown, it is difficult to see why children in real life should copy mass media aggressive heroes. The best explanation would lie in the process of identification which has already been refuted.

This section on imitation should not be concluded without reference to real life events which occasionally appear in the press indicting the mass media for various deviant behaviour. Such cases are of essentially two sorts. The first is the confession which provides a large number of the 'facts' condemning television in Mary Whitehouse's book.[38] Here individuals accused of criminal assaults and other nefarious activities sometimes claim that they got the idea from television. Such self-confessions have at times formed evidence even in psychological research. However, it was soon realised that these kinds of statements can often be interpreted as reflecting motivational distortion of reality rather than a true picture of the real determinants of behaviour — drinking, bad company, or whatever. These explanations may have some validity but can be more reliably interpreted as an attempt to 'pass the buck' and a social scientist would normally request more objective data than this.

The second type of case which occurs in the press is one where a criminal activity has followed some similar event in the mass media. Two cases of suicide apparently following patterns described on television were reported in Chapter 1. In part the reason for rejecting this type of evidence lies in the approach of scientists. Non-systematic investigation of natural phenomena can result in the identification of events as causing other events when in reality they merely precede them *(post hoc ergo propter hoc)*. The temptation to believe in causality when events precede and succeed each other results in the kinds of superstitious behaviour shown by sportsmen and gamblers. Cricketers will spit on a cricket ball, for example, or ritualistically toss it three times in the air before bowling. Apart from this problem of causality there is a more serious issue of representativeness of this kind of data. In a sense such case histories which impute preceding events on television are very much like the predictions of astrologers. When such predictions prove true they are sometimes of dramatic interest and can be quite striking — sufficiently newsworthy to make them reportable in the daily press. Unfortunately, for every case which is reported there are an inestimable number of failures. In all such cases one can never know whether the prediction or connection between one fictional event and one real event is completely accidental or not. Certainly, whenever rigorous scientific investigation has been directed to such phenomena, the evidence suggests that the apparent relationship is merely accidental.

Milgram and Shotland have reported a series of eight major studies of the effects of modelled behaviours in the mass media on imitation in the audience. These behaviours included theft and abusive telephone calls. Despite the fact that these studies used potential sample sizes of millions, in certain cases, no evidence was found to impute that the media were having adverse effects. This is not to say that the media do not encourage certain forms of behaviour ('streaking' may be a case in point at the time of writing) but there is no solid evidence to suggest that violence in the media is imitated in the way that some researchers would have us believe.

TRIGGERING

We have already rejected the evidence from criminal confessions and the infrequent case histories of acts which seem to mirror the content of the mass media. Having done so there remains little evidence to suggest that the mass media may 'trigger off' the unstable mind to bizarre action. That this is a common assumption was clear from the introductory chapters and that it is scientifically unacceptable is equally clear. To our knowledge there is but one study which tests any of the essential elements of the triggering hypothesis. The bulk of experimental studies have concentrated on normal individuals — university students and the like — with no emphasis on the emotionally disturbed individual. Walters and Willows[39] observed the effects of watching aggressive film models on disturbed and non-disturbed children. Although schizophrenic children were excluded, the clinical diagnoses of the disturbed boys included 'character', 'behaviour', and 'personality' disorders. The non-disturbed group were selected on the basis of not having any personality disturbances as judged by their headmaster. A brief video film of a female model acting aggressively towards various toys, or a control film in which the model did not act aggressively, was shown. The total number of aggressive and non-aggressive acts exhibited by the child when playing with similar toys to the model served as the measure of aggression.

In complete opposition to what the triggering hypothesis would suggest, it was found that the disturbed children imitated the aggressive behaviour of the model less frequently than the non-disturbed children. This can scarcely be a convenient finding for the proponents of the triggering hypothesis but, as we have already noted, these modelling experiments are not easily generalised to real life circumstances.

One of the advantages of the triggering hypothesis is that, at face value, it seems to explain why individuals should be bizarre enough to copy not very adaptive behaviours from the mass media. If a child kills another child and suggests that he did so because he had seen a similar event on television, one would like to assume — because 'normal' individuals don't behave in this way — that the child is odd. This is a very poor sort of explanation which has little to offer by way of enriching our understanding of the reasons why people act 'oddly'. Unfortunately the methods of science often cannot cope adequately with causal processes in single isolated circumstances such as the examples of 'triggering' can be assumed to be. Since by their nature the methods available for inferring causal relationships depend on events occurring with considerable frequency, rare events cannot be studied successfully using experimental methods.

Although Walters and Willows' study hints at the inadequacy of the triggering hypothesis, it is difficult to accept the study as the final arbiter here since the measure of aggression used was trivial and the situation rather different to those to which 'triggering' has been applied, even though their consideration of maladjusted children is timely.

DESENSITISATION

As we have explained, the precise meaning of this concept is rather obscure. Although it has been considered by some that, for example, the news coverage of the Vietnam war potentially had this effect on the American nation,[40] the term remains vague. One can to some extent understand the source of the concern in view of some fairly common assumptions about the causes of aggression. Some would consider the lack of compassion of the aggressor for the victim as a cause, others would assume that pilots are able to bomb vast civilian populations because they do not suffer the emotional consequences of facing the victim, and the ethnologist Konrad Lorenz has argued that the tendency of modern weapons to distance the aggressor from the victim effectively neutralises certain inhibitions against aggression.[41] As we saw in the previous chapter, the experimental evidence on this matter from studies of the effects of awareness of the suffering of the victim in connection with vicarious aggression is conflicting. However the question of whether there is any *prima facie* evidence for the desensitisation hypothesis still warrants some attention.

Berger[42] has shown that in adults emotional response (as measured by the galvanic skin response) to the witnessing of electric shocks given to a victim decreases after repeated exposure to the procedure. Lazarus and various colleagues[43] have shown that emotional response to a bloody and painful primitive ritual markedly decreases with prolonged exposure to the stimulus. Cline *et al.*[44] have shown that heavy viewers of TV have less physiological response to television programmes than infrequent viewers. It is very likely that this process of habituation does occur for mass media violence just as it occurs in connection with any other emotional response, but the social consequences of this are unclear.

It seems clear that desensitisation tends to be highly specific to those stimuli which are repeatedly shown and does not generalise to other stimuli.[45] Averill found that desensitisation was obtained for certain film excerpts but not to the rest of the film when it was later shown in total. Similarly, in an American Commission on Obscenity and Pornography study, over three weeks American college students spent one and a half hours each day alone in a room containing a great deal of visual and textual erotic material as well as non-erotic material such as *Reader's Digest.* The level of sexual arousal was measured by self-reports and by physiological measures such as penis volume, urinary acid phosphates and rate of heartbeat. The time spent reading or viewing erotic materials decreased rapidly over time as did the level of physiological response to these materials. Even when new materials were introduced at a much later date the arousal and interest of this experimental group was much lower than a control group of individuals not previously exposed to this massive dose of erotica. This study clearly shows that the process of affective satiation to mass media materials occurs even in the case as such a powerful drive as sex. The interesting and significant fact that emerged was that the satiation was specific to the media materials — there was no tendency for the satiation to generalise to the respondents' own sexual activities! If this could be extended to the mass media coverage of violence there would be no cause for concern over the undesirable consequences of desensitisation to media violence.

There is a modicum of evidence which is not incompatible with the American Commission's findings to suggest that exposure to mass media violence has no effect on emotional response to violence. In a study of the relationship between exposure to the mass media and attitudes to aggression, Howitt included an item intended to deal with the relationship between exposure and emotional response to aggression. The children in this study were asked the following question:

If you found an elderly woman after she had been beaten unconscious by thugs, how would you feel? Angry, Frightened, Disgusted, Ashamed, Joyful, Excited, Sympathetic, Distressed.[46]

The respondents were allowed to circle as many responses as they wished and the data were analysed in several ways. First of all the sum of the appropriate emotional responses to the situation was calculated from the angry, frightened, disgusted, sympathetic, and distressed responses while, similarly, an inappropriate emotional responses score was calculated on the basis of the number of joyful and excited responses each subject made. In addition, the individual affective responses were analysed separately. The two composite measures of affect (total appropriate and total inappropriate) revealed no significant relationships other than that girls and older children tended to give more appropriate emotional responses than boys and younger children. The data on the correlations of mass media exposure indexes with the individual affects is more striking. Although there were correlations between such individual affects as anger, disgust, excitement, and distress and various of the media exposure indexes used in this study, they were essentially in the negative direction. That is, the more one watched television the more appropriate responses one would feel in a real life situation. Excitement, perhaps an inappropriate response in that one should not be excited by the suffering of an old woman, was associated with watching fewer aggressive programmes and with low total weekly television viewing. Clearly this study gives us no reason to assert that desensitisation or habituation by the media could be a social problem. This conclusion is reinforced by the American Pornography Commission finding described above.

On the other hand, the issue of densitisation has scarcely been tackled by mass communications researchers and one would not wish to deny the possible consequences of such a process for society. One might have hoped that more research had been forthcoming on the question but the evidence to date is fairly coherent in its rejection of the presumed adverse consequences of habituation to repeated presentation of violence.

ATTITUDE CHANGE

Without doubt the most researched function of the mass media has been their persuasive properties; not that the mass media have been shown to have a profound influence on people's attitudes (the bulk of the evidence suggests that the mass media have very little influence on

81

the most dearly held values of an individual) but there is a considerable amount of evidence to suggest that in limited spheres of experience the mass media are persuasive.[4 7] The major reason for concentrating on attitude change in the present context is that the process is the one most closely related to how one would guess the media had their effects. Since the aggressive and violent material exhibited in the mass media is complex and hardly unequivocal, it would seem reasonable to suppose that any effect of vicarious violence would be mediated through very complex cognitive processes. After all, the socialising influence of the mass media could scarcely be akin to house-training a puppy. If the media do teach a message about aggression, it is necessary for the child to abstract what the message is. As content analysis has shown, the thematic content of media productions and the rewards and punishments for aggression are very complicated.[4 8] This suggests how important the intervening process of attitude formation and change would be in the relationship between the child and the media. It is not simply a question of the child succumbing to the message of the media; it is necessary for him to try to extract from the confusing array of images presented some sort of coherent synthesis of the plethora of messages. Even if the integration is achieved it remains problematic as to whether it will persuade him.

In laboratory experiments it is relatively easier to achieve coherency in the message advocated because one is concerned with the effects of relatively simple stimuli and not the complexities of an evening's or lifetime's viewing. Researchers have tended to ignore the possibility of using experimental methods to tackle the problem and have concentrated merely on the correlational approach; not that the experimental methods have been totally ignored but simply that survey techniques have been relatively over-represented in the literature. The experimental and survey study methodologies will be discussed separately in this connection.

SURVEY STUDIES

It might be suggested that for a correlational study of the relationship between viewing aggression and attitude to have the best chance of adequately assessing the effects of vicarious aggression on attitudes, the following factors should be incorporated:[4 9]

1. Since the media may be putting over all manner of messages about the utility of aggression, before attempting to discover whether the child has adopted these messages, it is essential to discover what these messages might be. It would after all be pointless to ask whether the media influence attitudes to birth control if there was no coverage in any way of birth control in the media. For the child to be influenced by a message, the message has to be transmitted in the media. Obviously the discovery of this, in itself, is a sizeable

study, and suggests the importance of content analysis. Ideally the sort of content analysis relevant to this would be dependent on the children's own perceptions of the content of the media, and not on the conceptions imposed by the researcher and interpreted by his adult assistants. There has been much work done on the content analysis of mass media portrayals of violence but little or none of this work has used the perceptions of young people. One exception is the work of Cumberbatch[50] who found that young people's perceptions of television content were reasonably in accord with the descriptions of television fare presented by content analysts.

2. There should be a close correspondence between the content of the media and the content of the measures used to evaluate the relationship between the mass media and attitude. The reasons for this are obvious and revolve around the assumption that media content should be more likely to influence attitudes relevant to that content than attitudes fairly irrelevant to that content. In a sense this is merely an extension of the first point. Although it is possible that the effects of a persuasive communication generalise to less relevant responses, one would be more convinced of a causal relationship if it could be shown that there is a one-to-one relationship, than if attitudes less relevant to media content correlate more highly with exposure.

These are not unreasonable requirements but scarcely any studies have been conducted which meet them. Certainly the often-quoted work of Lovibond[51] in no way meets these requirements. This study was carried out in Australia using several different media including television, radio, cinema, and comics. Arguing from the premise that mass media content is essentially Fascist in that it emphasises force and violence in an idolatry fashion and with sufficient coherence to be labelled an ideological system, Lovibond constructed a scale of Fascist attitudes which he correlated with mass media exposure in a sample of young adolescent boys. Broadly speaking, exposure to all of the different media correlated significantly with the measure of Fascist attitudes (the Children's F-Scale as it was called) with the exception of radio. Lovibond concluded on the basis of these findings that exposure to the mass media influences children in the direction of acceptance of the ideology measured by the Children's F-Scale. If the results are taken at their face value they give us cause for concern, although we do not know if the attitude would be related to action.

However, the data is far from being as strong as Lovibond supposes. One central problem is the relationship between the content of the attitude scale and the content of the mass media. Psychometrically the scale seems to be acceptable, but this is not necessarily a sign that it is valid for our purposes. Not much of the scale seems to reflect the content of the mass media. For example, it is difficult to imagine that the rather conservative media in Australia would put over programmes, the content of which would cause a boy to agree with the statement 'If I got the chance and knew I wouldn't get caught, I'd love to tie a girl up to a tree and whip her', or 'A boy ought to give his girl a slap now and then to keep her in line'. The relationship of these items to media content would seem somewhat tenuous — which would make us cautious of asserting anything on the basis of this data.

Further, many of the items used in this study have little if anything to do with aggression. For example, included amongst those items which correlate best with the total scale score are 'Women drivers aren't as good as men and never will be', 'A girl who hasn't got a good figure can't expect boys to be interested in her', 'Asians, and especially Chinese, aren't to be trusted', and 'Chaps who pinch cars for a joy-ride are only out for a bit of fun and you have to admit they've got nerve'. None of these items would seem to be measuring attitudes to aggression, although the scale does contain other items which do seem to be related to aggressive behaviour.

Such details as these make it difficult to believe that the scale is measuring what it purports to be measuring and that the relationship between the media exposure indexes and the Children's F-Scale score is all that it appears to be. Certainly one would not assume the scale to be measuring aggressive attitudes on the basis of its content alone and one would not consider that its content could realistically tap the effects of television content either.[52]

Hartmann and Husband[53] have pointed to what would seem to be the fundamental flaw in the study, and a very simple one at that. Lovibond describes his sample as consisting of boys selected to give a sample representative of Adelaide metropolitan schoolboys of 11-15 years of age. Given this one would suppose that the researcher would have controlled for social class variation within the sample. Since social class is known to predict amount of media exposure and to correlate with Fascist attitudes, the correlation between Lovibond's measure of Fascism and extent of media exposure may well be an artifact of the failure to control for essential confounding variables.

Howitt[54] carried out a study which attempted to overcome many of the difficulties in Lovibond's study, especially those bearing on the relationship between the mass media and aggressive attitudes. The study was designed bearing in mind the considerations of how such an ideal study should be conducted. The work was therefore based on content analysis and the attitudes measured were relevant to the content of the mass media. The content analysis was essentially the work of George Gerbner as interpreted by Baker and Ball.[55] These authors, on the basis of material collected through the methods of content analysis, suggest that the mass media preach a number of messages related to aggression. For example, they argue that because those who commit violence in the mass media are usually youngish and unmarried, then the mass media communicate the message that unmarried young to middle-aged males are usually violent. Although the assumption has to be made that the results of the content analysis can be interpreted as implying children's perceptions, an assumption for which there is little empirical support, it seems reasonable to suppose that this comes nearer to the ideal than the conventional methodology, despite the obvious limitations of the procedures.

The study used a wide variety of television exposure indexes including ones for both fictional and documentary programmes. The list was, in full, the total number of aggressive programmes viewed, the total number of news programmes viewed, the total number of cartoon programmes viewed, weighted total number of aggressive programmes (weighted to make allowance for frequency of viewing), weighted total number of news programmes viewed, weighted total number of cartoon programmes, total weekly television viewing, total number of years of television at home, total number of current favourite television programmes of an aggressive nature, and total number of favourite aggressive programmes. This wide variety helped cover the broad gamut of possible media socialising influences, from early history of television viewing to the amount of exposure to news programmes (which, of course, contain quite frequent references to violence).

The aggressive attitudes questions varied markedly in their format from fixed choice to open ended types. Because it was not expected that aggressive attitudes would be highly intercorrelated and because it was not felt to be essential that attitudes should be measured using lengthy scales, all of the items were analysed individually and no attempt was made to form scales from them. It is worth mentioning that the traditional criteria in social science for constructing attitude scales emphasise unidimensionality which makes the items finally selected somewhat similar. This procedure is incompatible with attempts to measure a very broad attitude area. Since there is no reason to assume that the media should concentrate on just one particular attitude area, it is best to take as wide an approach as possible. Hypotheses tested included the influence of the medium on the probability that the child would resolve conflict by the use of violence, that he would probably use violence as a means to achieve desired ends, that he would probably passively observe violence between others, that he would regard policemen as being violent, that he would develop more positive attitudes towards violence as a means of fulfilment of individual ends, have an attitude that young men can enhance their masculinity by displaying proficiency in the use of violence, have a lowered valuation of non-violent means of problem solving, develop the attitude that it is not the responsibility of individual citizens to help each other out of violent situations, and so forth. An example or two of the attitude items used will go some way to clarifying the procedures. It is important to remember that the respondents were young adolescent boys and girls. The assertion that those socialised by mass media violence would probably passively observe violence between others was tested by the item 'If you found two boys fighting in the school playground, what would you do?' to which the children had to write a few sentences to explain what action they would take in these circumstances. These replies were coded to indicate the extent to which the child would in some way intervene (e.g. break the fight up or go and fetch a teacher). In order to test the possibility that television encourages the attitude that young men can enhance their masculinity by displaying proficiency in the use of violence the following item was used: 'John Smith is always ready for a fight. He does not take rudeness from anybody. He acts big and tough all of the time. How manly (masculine) would you say that John Smith is?' This question was followed by a five point scale ranging from Very unmanly, Unmanly, Neither manly nor unmanly, Manly, to Very manly.

The correlations between the exposure indexes and the measures of aggressive attitudes were by and large near zero. In fact, the number of significant correlations actually obtained are explicable on the basis of chance alone. The number of significant correlations was even further reduced when possible confounding variables such as sex, age, class, sibling order, and family size had been partialled out. Howitt suggests that out of sixteen hypotheses put forward by Baker and Ball and tested in this study, all but three could be rejected on the basis of the empirical findings. This is not to say that these three hypotheses received much support at all but only that they could not be completely discounted. These three possible hypotheses are:

1. Persons socialised by the media 'if they were policemen, would be likely to meet violence with violence, often escalating its level'.
2. Distinctions between fantasy and reality presentations of media violence are not consistently perceived by child audiences (and this varies with socialisation influences).
3. That television socialises children to the view that problems should be tackled by immediate action.

In total these findings give us little cause for concern. The first hypothesis really concerns the child's perceptions of a situation or role which is basically outside of his everyday experience. Although this in a sense is serious, it certainly would not necessarily imply anything about the child's aggressive behaviour. Whether or not solving problems by immediate action is a bad thing is a value judgement and does not, of course, mean that the action will be aggressive. The relationship between exposure and perceptions of the difference between reality and fantasy seems unlikely to be due to the effects of exposure but due to some prior disposition. The findings are almost diametrically opposed to some assertions made in the U.S. Surgeon General's report.

There are two studies in this report which are directly related to the issue at hand. These are by J. Dominick and B. Greenberg[56] and by McLeod, Atkin and Chaffee.[57] Of these the Dominick and Greenberg study provides the least persuasive support for the relationship between aggressive attitudes and violent television. Their study made use of three variables which were felt to have a likely effect on aggressive attitudes: these were exposure to television violence, the perceived attitudes of the family to aggression, and social class. Each of these variables was thought to have an individual effect on aggressive attitudes and each of them would tend to interact with the others to produce an even greater effect. These are called interaction effects. Exposure to television violence consisted of the number of aggressive television programmes watched each week and the four measures of aggressive attitudes used were as follows:

1. Approval of violence: These items were taken and modified from Sears' measure of anti-social aggression. Examples are 'I see nothing wrong in a fight between two teenage boys' and 'It's all right if a man slaps his wife'.

2. Willingness to use violence. These were items taken from another established psychological inventory called the Buss-Durkee Hostility inventory. An example of the items used is 'Anybody who says bad things about me is looking for a punch on the nose'.

3. Perceived effectiveness of violence: These were original items designed to elucidate how much the child felt violence was an effective means of solving problems. Examples given are 'Sometimes a fight is the easiest way to get what you want' or 'A fight is the best way to settle an argument once and for all'.

4. Suggested solutions to conflict situations: This consisted of open-ended questions to which the child gave an indication of what he would do in potentially frustrating situations. Questions included 'Pretend somebody you know takes something from you and breaks it on purpose. What would you do?' and 'Pretend somebody you know tells lies about you. What would you do?'

The sample used in this study were over 800 boys and girls of roughly 10 to 12 years of age. Boys' and girls' results were analysed separately thus cutting out the risk of a sex artifact.

In general, for both boys and girls, there tended to be a significant association between aggressive viewing and exposure to television violence, family attitudes to violence, and social class. There tended to be some interaction between exposure and parental attitudes, but the bulk of the association between the three variables failed to interact to give better predictions. While this is some sort of evidence for asserting a relationship between exposure and attitude it is very difficult to evaluate

87

the extent to which this assertion should be given credence on the basis of these findings. For example, since it is shown in this study that social class is a powerful predictor of attitudes and because we can assume that class and television exposure correlate, it is surprising that Dominick and Greenberg do not report the effects of partialling (i.e. controlling for) out this variable in their analysis. After all, family attitudes to aggression might both influence exposure and attitudes and so should be controlled for. All of this is not to say that exposure to television violence does not cause these attitudes, but simply that on the basis of this evidence we cannot be sure, and that consequently the evidence says little.

Greenberg's related study of British children[59] is a virtual repetition of the American study. Seven hundred and twenty-six children between the age 9-15 took part in the study. Aggressive attitudes were correlated significantly with violence viewing and non-violence viewing. The correlation remains significant even when non-violence viewing is partialled out of the relationship between violence viewing and aggressive attitudes. Since it is impossible to explain how non-violent programmes can influence aggressive attitudes on any model of socialisation, the inadequacy of these studies is further confirmed.

The McLeod, Atkin and Chaffee study[59] is beset with similar problems, although here more attention was paid to controlling spurious associations than in the previous research. The study involved two samples of children. One consisted of 229 thirteen-year-olds and 244 sixteen-year-olds while the other consisted of 225 adolescents apparently roughly comparable in age to the members of the first sample. Boys and girls were included in both. The measures of aggressive attitudes used were as follows:

1. Manifest physical aggression. This was partly adapted from the Buss-Durkee aggression-hostility inventory and partly from the work of Greenberg and Dominick. The items included 'If somebody hits me first, I let him have it' and 'When I am mad at someone, I sometimes fight with them instead of talking about the problem'.

2. Aggressive behavioural delinquency: These items were taken from Short and Nye's delinquency scale and were 'Been in fights with several people on each side', 'Hurt someone on purpose to get back for something they had done to you' 'Got into a serious fight with another student at school'.

3. Zaks-Walters Aggression: These items were taken from the Zaks-Walters scale and included 'I often do things which I regret after, I am very patient with people' (reversed for scoring purposes), and 'There are two kinds of people in this world: the weak and the strong'.

4. Hypothetical aggressive reactions. Here the children were presented with four hypothetical conflict situations and asked to choose among three or four alternatives the thing they were most likely to

do. Examples given include 'What if someone cut in front of you in a long line. What would you do to them?' and 'Suppose someone played a real dirty trick on you. What would you do?'

A further measure was developed which was a composite of all of the above sorts of items. The measure of television exposure was frequency of viewing aggressive programmes.

The preliminary runs on the data revealed two very important trends. First of all that 'boys show considerably higher levels on most aggression measures than do girls' and that 'there is a considerable decline in aggression level from junior to senior high on most indices'. Boys have more aggressive attitudes than girls while older children have less aggressive attitudes. Further, there seems to be a trend for the viewing patterns to exhibit a similar relationship. In terms of overall violence viewing, the younger child seems to watch more than the older child, the male watching more than the female. These findings are very important because they show the need to control for both sex and age in such studies. This is made even clearer in the analysis of the data. While for both samples and for all the measures of aggressive attitudes (except for Zaks-Walters aggression measure for the larger sample) there were significant positive correlations between television violence exposure and aggressive attitudes, this is misleading since, when for each measure four sub-groups were formed on the basis of age and sex, the number of significant associations was found to be relatively low and some of the original correlations were clearly due to artifacts of sex and age. For the larger sample only 10 of the possible 20 correlations between attitude and viewing were significant, while for the smaller sample only 2 of the 20 possible correlations were significant. Clearly these figures reduce considerably our confidence that the original correlations suggest causal relationships between exposure and attitude.

There is another important point to bear in mind. Two different samples of children were used in this study — one the Wisconsin sample, the other the Maryland sample. In a sense this gives us a measure of the reliability of the findings. Since we can presume that the effects of television violence should be roughly the same in every part of the country, if we do not get the same correlations from sample to sample we must be very dubious about the assertions of any study. This is particularly true of Chaffee and McLeod's findings. There were twenty different correlations between television violence and the measures of aggression, many of which were significant (up to about half in fact) for each sample, but *only one of these partial correlations out of the twenty was statistically significant for both the Wisconsin and Maryland samples!* Clearly one would find this difficult to explain in terms of the media-cause-violence assertion.

None of these studies can be taken as definitive statements of the effects of mass media violence on aggressive attitudes. We have seen that it is necessary to control for a whole array of different sorts of confounding variables before satisfactory conclusions can be reached, and that for many the reported correlations between exposure and attitude become insignificant when such variables as sex, age and the like are taken into consideration. Ultimately, with any correlational study, it is impossible to know whether the confounding variables have all been partialled out, and for this reason it is essential to take experimental studies into account. Because of the difficulty in correlational studies of finally proving 'effects' we must now turn our attention to experimental studies of the effects of the mass media on attitudes to aggression.

Experimental Studies:

Experimental studies of the relationship between aggressive attitudes and exposure to mass media violence are few and far between. In fact there have been only two major studies dealing with such relationships. The reasons for this are fairly obvious, the principle one being that since ultimately our concern is with the effects of media exposure on behaviour and since attitudinal measures at best can tell us about a possible intervening process between exposure and action, it is far better to concentrate on the question of exposure/behaviour rather than exposure/attitude which would leave us one step removed from the type of answer we are interested in.

Heinrich[60] was the first researcher to carry out a major experimental study of the effects of exposure to aggressive films on the attitudes of the adolescent viewer. The film materials were shown individually and the child's response to them measured. There was no question of using long-term exposure to the film material as the basis of the study. The methodology involved a pre-test measure of attitudes, personal details, and reactions to the film followed by exposure to the film, followed by a post-test measure of aggression attitudes. While there were two forms of the questionnaires which were to be administered before and after the film — i.e. two versions of a sentence scale of aggressive attitudes — it appears that the alternative forms were not counterbalanced in presentation and that the same alternative of the two was given at each pre-test and post-test session. That is, Form A was given for the pre-test and Form B was given for the post-test in every case. Because one cannot assume that the two alternative forms are in fact equivalent, it is usual in pre- and post-test designs to counterbalance orders of presentation of the dependent measure so as to introduce a control for such inequalities in the measuring instruments. The meaning of the changes is difficult to interpret because of this failure.

The films included in this study were *Bad Day at Black Rock, Blackboard Jungle, Snow White, Hell-Cats of the Navy, Johnny on the Run, Powder River,* and a number of German films making a total of twelve in all. All the films were in German tongue because the subjects were young adolescent Germans. There was no simple trend for all of the films to produce an increase or decrease in aggressive attitudes in the viewer. The measures of aggressive attitudes used were fairly straight-forward and included such items as 'If someone lets the air out of my tyres I'm obliged to do the same to him. Every blow I receive is returned immediately. It's better to give way to someone spoiling for a fight. I cannot bear a slur on my honour; I must avenge it. There are cases where you can't very easily renounce revenge, and you pay back insults with interest' (the stiffness of the language is due to our translation).

Those films which did seem to produce an increase in aggressive attitudes seem to be rather different to those which produced no change or even a decrement. Heinrich argues that in general films 'have the effect of increasing aggressiveness if the theme of aggression is handled in a heavy, dynamic and realistic way, the film enabling an identification with people who decide on aggression in a conflict situation.' The only film which seemed to cause a significant reduction in aggressiveness was *Snow White* which Heinrich says was distinguished from the other films in that it is 'a fairy tale produced realistically, following a peaceful course, it illustrates material familiar from childhood onwards, omitting some of the more gruesome details, and it gives the opportunity for identification, supplemented by a contrary identification'. Since the film of *Peter Pan* produced no such decrement, it cannot be that the fairy tale element alone produced this trend.

Although it is not fruitful to suggest reasons why films should increase aggressive attitudes, on the basis of the available evidence here, it seems unlikely, from our earlier discussion,[61] that it is actual exposure to an aggressive hero with whom the audience can identify which produces this effect. In fact, because the study did not involve control groups not exposed to any film at all, it is difficult to know whether aggressive films increase attitudes to aggression or simply decrease them relatively less than other sorts of film. The problems involved in collection of pre-test/post-test measures mentioned above compound this difficulty. One certainly could not preclude some sort of effect on the basis of this data alone, however.

Since it seems that aggressive films do not necessarily influence the aggressiveness of the attitudes of the viewer, it is worthwhile asking what is the effect of repeated exposure to different sorts of aggressive films. The most important ramification of this is the question of the effects of mass media television programmes on aggressive attitudes. One important study is that of Feshbach and Singer.[62] This study is critical in that it was carried out in naturalistic conditions and random assignment to viewing conditions was instigated. Half of the adolescent boys watched a diet rich in violence for six weeks while the other group watched a non-aggressive television diet. More details are given in the preceding chapter where the methodology of this study is covered in detail. The dependent measure of attitudes towards aggression involved both attitudes to interpersonal aggression and attitudes towards public policy and generalisations about aggressive behaviour. Included on the interpersonal scale were such items as 'It is very seldom right to hit another person', while the public policy scale included the item 'Teenage hoodlums should be punished severely'. Essentially the study concluded that aggressive attitudes tended to be highest in those groups exposed to non-aggressive television fare and lowest in the experimental group exposed to violent television fare — quite the reverse of what would be expected on the basis of the media-cause-violence hypothesis. It would seem that if the media teach anything about aggressive values it is that non-aggression is to be preferred.

While not a truly experimental design, it is worthwhile noting in the present context the findings of Schramm, Lyle, and Parker[63] about the relationship between television and aggressive attitudes. In this study the children of a town in which television had been introduced were compared with those of a non-television town, as closely matched as possible, on Sears' measures of aggressive attitude. There was no tendency for those children in the television town to have higher aggressive attitude scores than those children from the radio town. This supports Feshbach and Singer's findings. Indeed, in the data there are only three significant differences. Two of these are in the direction of lower anti-social aggression in the teletown groups. The third difference is in aggression anxiety where the teletown group was higher. In other words, children show less aggressive attitudes and suffer more anxiety about the use of aggression when they are exposed to television.

Menzies[64] carried out a simple laboratory type experiment on the effects of filmed violence and found differences, apparently due to the films, in aggressive attitudes. But a correlational study using similar measures and a similar sample failed to support these findings.

There is no simple statement which can present an adequate summary of these various findings. It has been shown that where attitudinal content and television content are closely matched there is little evidence of any adverse influence of the media on children's attitudes. However, where the researchers have not taken this elementary precaution of matching the contents, there has tended to be a correlation between exposure to mass media violence and attitudes to aggression. Despite the fact that it has been shown that these associations can be partly explained as artifacts of the correlational methodology, the complete list of confounding variables has not been found and the possibility of a causal influence of the media alone cannot be excluded on this basis. However, when we turn to the experimental literature on the relationship between the media and attitudes to aggression, it becomes clear that the most substantial studies indicate no consistent relationship or even an unexpected lowering of aggressive attitudes due to exposure to mass media violence. It seems possible for the mass media to influence attitudes adversely, but there is no evidence that this potential is realised.

We have other reasons for doubting the adverse influence of the mass media in this area. First of all, the weight of the evidence on the effects of the mass media suggests that they are most influential in areas of ill-formed attitudes.[65] Since aggression is one of the most central issues in socialisation, it would be unlikely that the media could operate effectively in the face of family processes and the like. Nevertheless, it might seem more feasible that attitudes rather than behaviour would be changed by media exposure. Even so, the evidence which exists reveals that there is very little to suggest that attitude change is manifested in behavioural change. For example, Festinger[66] has reviewed what little evidence there is in favour of the assertion that attitude change results in behavioural change and found little to support the presumed association.

Another important issue is whether attitudes are in fact valid predictors of behaviour at all. Children may hold a particular attitude for all sorts of reasons and there is no necessary reason to assume that it will have any relationship with overt behaviour. For example, in a small pilot study Friedman and Johnson found evidence of the basic invalidity of certain measures. A group of aggressive boys (as selected by school counsellors and the vice-principal in charge of discipline) was matched with a control group of boys not possessing aggressive tendencies. The researchers compared the responses of the aggressive and non-aggressive boys to attitude scales. The researchers noted:

> The various psychological inventories used in this research effort failed to distinguish with satisfactory validity between the aggressive and non-aggressive boys. The experimenters hoped that this pre-test would provide a base for developing a short scale of optimal reliability and validity which could be used to relate personal aggressiveness to the viewing of violent television content. Of the 85 items drawn from various scales, less than ten elicited substantial response differences between aggressives and non-aggressives. Items from the scales with widest use, those of Buss-Durkee and Sears, fared less well than those from other sources.[67]

Faced with such problems of interpretation of attitude scores, it is necessary to consider the issues very carefully before imputing the worst about the effects of mass media violence on aggressive attitudes. Certainly there is no unanimous conclusion to be drawn from the assertions of the researchers. Despite the fact that the experimental literature has tended to suggest a nil or negative effect, in the main, of exposure to mass media violence, at face value the correlational research is less clear cut. Part of this association is due to uncontrolled factors. While ultimately it is wrong to deny the possibility of a link, the most reasonable conclusion to draw on the basis of the available evidence is that attitude change cannot represent a process whereby violence on television causes violence in society.

GENERAL CONCLUSION

Imitation, identification, triggering, desensitisation, and attitude change have all been popular contenders as processes which could link mass media violence exposure with aggressive behaviours in society. Identification, triggering, and desensitisation seem to have little or no support in the empirical literature and can, with some certainty, be ruled out. Imitation, on the other hand, has received considerable attention in the literature and has often been thought to mediate the effects of media exposure. At first sight there is considerable evidence that there is a link since young children have often been observed, under laboratory conditions, to replicate the aggressive behaviour of a filmed model. The difficulty with this sort of study is knowing the validity of the dependent measures as correlates of real life aggressive behaviour. While striking an inflated plastic clown may well seem to be aggressive it also would seem to bear the essential characteristics of play behaviour. Certainly the evidence is suggestive of the measure's basic invalidity as a measure of aggression. Recent studies[68] have demonstrated that the child is willing to aggress against a man dressed up as a plastic clown after witnessing aggression against a plastic clown but it still remains likely that this is playful behaviour. Why should anyone dress up as a clown if not for fun? It has been shown that rewarding or punishing an aggressive model can have a substantial impact upon the relationship between exposure and modelling, the relevance of such studies to the effects of exposure to the mass media is very dubious. After all, without these studies it would not be in very much doubt that children can, if they wanted to, imitate aggression in the mass media and incorporate it in their own aggressive behaviour. The critical issue is whether or not the child performs the behaviour which is learned, not whether he learns it or not. Performing aggression copied from the screen in serious behaviour has rather different implications to punching a Bobo doll after seeing a filmed model perform such actions. The fact that the evidence suggests that imitation in the laboratory does not generalise very well to real life situations, if at all, would cause us to concern ourselves less and less with trying to answer real life problems on the basis of such studies.

Attitude change which at face value is a very likely process intervening between exposure and action or is probably not an important contributory mechanism for several reasons. Most important of these is the observation that attitude change has rarely been associated with behaviour change and that the exceptions to this rule deal with trivial attitudes. The empirical literature on the effects of the mass media is a little confusing. The experimental studies (in which spurious correlations caused by confounding variables are excluded) have tended to lead to rather different conclusions to the vast majority of the correlational studies where spurious variance receives less than perfect control. Another issue is whether the mass media can be expected to affect attitudes towards aggression which do not closely match the content of the media. The evidence seems to suggest that when a media content and attitude scale content are closely matched, little or no evidence of the effects of the media on attitudes emerges.

All in all it does not seem wide of the mark to suggest that there is little empirical evidence to implicate the intervening processes of attitude change, identification, imitation, triggering, and densensitisation, in the effects of mass media violence. To the extent that these processes can be excluded it increases our confidence in the assertion that media violence does not adversely affect people. However, this is not the sort of argument which can finally produce an answer to the question of effects. After all, there might be other processes through which the media might have their effect — or are there? The reader might like to put forward alternative proposals which can be tested against available data. The only major contenders have been dealt with in the previous chapter, i.e. cueing and catharsis. Since the evidence for these does not pass without dispute we can assert that the evidence for any of the intervening processes is in doubt and, consequently, their relevance to the issue at hand.

The next chapter is concerned with the correlational studies of the relationship between mass media exposure and aggressive or delinquent *behaviour.* A subcultural account of the adequate data emerging from this is put forward, which further suggests that the mass media do not cause aggression. Since these studies are more relevant to the practical problems of media violence they are well worth studying before reaching a conclusion.

CHAPTER FIVE
CORRELATIONAL FIELD
STUDIES

Numerous correlational field studies have investigated the relationship between the quantity of mass media exposure and either aggression or delinquency in the audience. Of course, as is often pointed out, such studies cannot tell us if the mass media actually *caused* the audience to be violent or delinquent since there are so many possible confounding variables which can provide alternative explanations of causal sequences in such relationships. An example of such spurious factors might be that since delinquents crave excitement both their delinquent activity and a liking for exciting television material are merely manifestations of the need for excitement. Alternatively, delinquents may imagine themselves as toughies and so prefer to view programmes containing tough and aggressive characters. One lesson of the present chapter is that simple and mundane contingencies such as sex and age often intervene to create an apparent relationship between exposure and delinquency.

Few, if any, correlational methodologists seem oblivious of the difficulties created by spurious variables, For example,

... no survey or correlational study which merely seeks to establish whether delinquents and non-delinquents differ in their media behaviour is in a position to offer proof or disproof about the suggested causal relationship between media content and deviant or lawbreaking behaviour.[1] or

The studies reviewed in this chapter indicate that a modest relationship exists between the viewing of violence on television and aggressive tendencies. Because all of the studies present correlational data, definitive conclusions about causal relationships cannot be drawn. The evidence reviewed here is consonant both with the interpretation that violence viewing leads to aggression to a limited degree and among a limited number of young people, and with the interpretation that both the viewing and the aggression are products of an as yet unidentified third variable. The data are also consonant with the interpretation that both these processes occur simultaneously.[2]

Anyone antagonistic to the spending of public funds on social science might feel somewhat alarmed by such statements. After all, why spend money on such research if it is known in advance that any findings are basically irrelevant to the question of the effects of the mass media? There seems to be little or no point in picking out a group such as delinquents for study if our concern is not with the effects of the mass media on delinquency.

Of course, things are not as simple as this and such studies can be justified in several ways. Most revolve around the problems of experimental research in this area, but some also draw on the view that if a phenomenon can or cannot be demonstrated correlationally then this constitutes preliminary evidence for or against further action. Basic to this sort of argument is the assumption, as it happens unwarranted, that even a spurious correlation between television and aggression will lead to a conservative policy decision which ensures that the possible undesirable effects of media violence are avoided. An example of this sort of argument comes from the report of United States government investigators:

Non-experimental studies have definite strengths. They do measure things as they actually occur — in all their variety, profusion, and complexity. They can falsify the applicability of hypotheses to real life; for example, if violence viewing and aggressiveness proved not to be associated, concern over causal links in either direction could be abandoned.[3]

The difficulty with this is that it implies that spurious, uncontrolled variables which can influence the correlation between aggression and mass media exposure tend to produce an artifactual positive correlation. In fact spurious correlation coefficients can be positive, negative, or zero depending upon the direction and size of the correlations between the two variables of interest and the third, confounding variable. This is true no matter whether in reality vicarious aggression has a stimulating, a cathartic, or no effect on the viewer's subsequent aggressive tendencies.

Despite this argument, it remains imperative to explore the correlational studies of the relationship between the mass media and violence in society. Whereas correlation studies have little or no status of proof of effects, they have often been interpreted, in conjunction with certain experimental findings, as providing support for the contention that media violence influences the level of violence in society. There is no necessary reason for supposing that both survey and experimental evidence are not equally artifactual but it is comfortable to assume that a relationship detected in radically different contexts by radically different procedures may be reflecting more than mere artifacts. In any case, the more there are correlational studies yielding essentially the same conclusion on the basis of radically different techniques, samples, and so forth, the more difficult it is to believe that these findings should not be considered seriously. It is assumed in this chapter that this argument has some cogency, but we prefer a rather different explanation of these correlational findings to that of the adverse effects of mass media aggression.

The primary concern of this section is the relationship between media exposure and *aggression* but many relevant studies have dealt with the concept of *delinquency* rather than aggression. We will discuss these somewhat different variables as if they were one partly because of the obvious overlap betwen the two (much of what is called delinquent behaviour also qualifies as aggressive behaviour and vice versa) but also because this leads to an interesting synthesis of the research literature. Our analysis also requires that we deal with each of the various mass media separately since the argument is that there is a different relationship between exposure to each of the various mass media and aggression or delinquency. We concentrate on behaviour rather than attitude (which was dealt with in the previous chapter) because the precise implications of attitudinal variables for social policy and their validity for scientific conclusions about the effects of the mass media are not clear.

A difficulty arises over the sorts of variables which can be considered as valid indicators of the socialising influence of the mass media. There are two broad classes of variable which seem relevant and have been considered in the research literature:

1. Measures of length of exposure (whether this is total viewing time, total aggressive programming, etc. is no matter).
2. Measures of gratifications obtained (e.g. the viewer's favourite sort of television programme, how much he likes aggressive programmes, and so forth).

Our preference is for the various sorts of duration of exposure measures, but clearly gratification variables have an appeal. Our discontent with the gratification measures is that their meaning is uncertain. For example, if someone says that he likes a Western series such as *The Virginian*, are we to take it that he will be more likely to be influenced by its content than someone who does not like the series? If the dislike of the series causes the individual to avoid watching the programme then it may influence the socialisation process but, on the other hand, the question remains whether liking interacts with watching to increase the probability that the individual will be socialised by the programme. There is no useful evidence to help us on this point.[4] There are many reasons why one would doubt the existence of any causal link if it were found that aggressive youngsters preferred aggressive programmes. They might like aggressive programmes because they are aggressive children and such programmes support their aggressive self-image. In any case, the laboratory studies of the effects of filmed aggression only rely on measures of exposure — an important point if we are to tackle the popular belief among social scientists that the evidence from both laboratory and field is unanimous in demonstrating the harmful effects of television violence. In addition the considerable element of uncertainty about what liking means gives further reason to favour measures of actual exposure. This is not to say that exposure to a programme and liking it are not related — the evidence demonstrates a relationship, albeit imperfect. Of course, the ideal measure would be that of actual exposure to violent programmes, an ideal which is reached in certain investigations.

The research described in this chapter spans a period of roughly fifty years — from the first integrated attempt by the Payne Fund to understand the role of the cinema in the lives of young people — until recent research such as that commissioned by the United States Surgeon General's Office on the effects of television. In many ways research has not changed much in the intervening years — perhaps the techniques and statistical treatment are a little more sophisticated now — but the essential problems of controlling confounding variables remain central. That the research spans such a long period may be an adverse reflection on the ability of our available research methods to deal with social problems but, from the point of view of the theoretical account of the findings to be presented, the relatively immense time-span only serves to emphasise the adequacy of our perspective.

TELEVISION

Television has been available as a truly mass medium for about twenty-five years. It has probably contributed more to the debate about the effects of the mass media than any other medium and its share of the research cake has been correspondingly large. This is not surprising in view of the enormous proportion of an individual's time which is devoted to it. The estimates vary, but it is not far wide of the mark to suggest that for the majority of people in the western world television occupies the major portion of their leisure time.[5] If this is not a cause for concern to social scientists, it is difficult to think what is. Children, equally, view an enormous amount of television and not surprisingly, some find it difficult to believe that they are unaffected by what they see on the screen.

Our review of the studies correlating television exposure with aggressiveness in the audience will begin with the study which, at face value, seems to demonstrate a possible adverse influence of the mass media. The authors of this study, Eron, Lefkowitz, and other colleagues,[6] are unusual in that they assert that their evidence, albeit correlational, can be interpreted as evidence for the adverse effects of television on aggressive behaviour. The study was itself part of a larger project on the determinants of aggression and covered a ten-year span. Children were studied at the age of eight or nine years and then again, when nearing adulthood, ten years afterwards. Aggression was measured by asking the class-mates of the children to guess who in the class fitted the descriptions implied in such questions is 'Who does not obey the teacher? Who often says, "Give me that!"? Who does things that bother others? Who starts a fight over nothing? Who pushes or shoves children? Who is always getting into trouble?' They used ten questions in all and it should not be overlooked that these questions, which were combined to give an overall aggression score, range far more widely than simple physical aggression and include a measure of assertive behaviour.

Exposure to television was measured by parental reports and included the number of hours the child was said to watch television as well as the parents' ratings of the child's favourite programmes. A violent programme preference score was calculated on the basis of independent ratings of the violence content of the children's favourite programmes as judged by two adults.

The results are intriguing. First of all there was no significant correlation for *girls* between the television exposure indexes and peer nominations of aggression. However, this did not hold true for boys since there was a *significant negative* relationship between television exposure and ratings of aggression but a *significant positive* relationship between preferences for aggressive programmes and nominations of aggression. That is, aggressive boys watch less television but prefer violent television programmes more compared with low aggressive boys.

The one clear conclusion stemming from these results is that exposure to the media as such would not be implicated in any assertions of harmful effects. However the relationship between programme preferences and aggression ratings in boys is paralleled by the lack of any such associations in girls. This makes interpretation difficult. It does, however, open up the possibility that whatever is causing the association of aggressiveness with liking violent programmes for boys is societal and not the result of the mass media. If the media make boys aggressive it is difficult to see why they do not make girls equally so. After all, laboratory studies have reached such a conclusion. One interpretation of the relationship (which was only found for the mother's ratings of favourite programmes) is that the mothers were oblivious to their children's viewing habits and that they had named programmes which fitted in with their conceptions of what aggressive boys might be expected to like.

However, the study also involved a later follow-up using as many respondents from the earlier study as could be contacted after stringent efforts had been made. At this later stage, aggressive television viewing was measured by asking the respondent for information rather than the parent and the peer ratings of aggression were gathered retrospectively since the children had left school. For some reason the researchers do not seem to think that such procedures are radically different from the original measures. The relationship between exposure and aggression at the age of eighteen or nineteen, unlike ten years previously, was insignificant (slightly negative in fact) but the level of aggressive viewing at the age of eight or nine was as powerful a predictor of aggressive behaviour at eighteen or nineteen as it was ten years previously. Since at the later date, the subject was asked to recall his classmates' behaviour when they were at school together, this may only go to show that aggressive youngsters are not readily forgotten.

This longitudinal study, although it at first seems to provide evidence for the adverse stimulating effects of television violence on a long term basis, cannot be taken at its face value. Certainly there is absolutely no evidence to suggest that exposure to television adversely influences aggressive behaviour (the opposite, if anything occurs) and the mother's perceptions of her son's favourite television programmes, as Kay suggests,[7] are likely to be pretty invalid. All in all, therefore, this study can scarcely by regarded as adequately demonstrating that television socialises youngsters into aggression.

Furthermore, an attempt by Milavsky to replicate this study with slight improvements in methodology, while succeeding in reproducing the level of the correlation between violence ratings and viewing habits, alerts us to a critical flaw in the correlation. Milavsky[8] incorporated into his questionnaire of media usage names of programmes which simply did not exist. Should anyone claim that he watched such programmes it could be reasonably assumed that he was an unreliable reporter. When the correlation between television use and peer ratings of aggression are computed, controlling for this factor of unreliability, the correlations become very much smaller and the adequacy of the original study by Eron et al is brought into question. While small relationships do remain it is possible that controlling for unreliability of reporting as a continuous variable (instead of as a dichotomous one) would obliterate the correlation entirely. Nevertheless, our confidence in the original study is shaken still further by this.

McLeod, Atkin and Chaffee[9] contributed a report to the U.S. Surgeon General's research programme which ostensibly demonstrated a strong correlation between violence viewing and overt aggressive behaviour. As in the Eron and Lefkowitz study, peer reports were used to measure each child's aggressiveness but television viewing was measured by the individual's own estimates. Teacher and mother reports of aggression were also gathered.

Every child (adolescent) in the sample had to rate ten of his classmates on three dimensions of aggression and irritability:
1. Patience with others (a negative measure of irritability).
2. Hits other people when loses temper (assault aggression).
3. Yelling back when yelled at (verbal aggression).
Responses to all three measures were summated to give an overall aggression score for each child. Several television exposure indexes were calculated, the most important being the total viewing time of the respondent and the total amount of violent programme viewing.

Taking first of all the correlations between total viewing time and level of aggressive behaviour reported by others, rather mixed findings are revealed. The teacher-report of general aggression did not correlate significantly with the total viewing time, and a similar lack of any relationship was apparent for the mother-reports of aggression. This pattern was matched by a number of measures such as self-report of verbal aggression, peer-report of verbal aggression, peer-report of irritability, approval of aggression, and aggressive attitudes. The only significant positive correlations of aggression with total television viewing time were those of the peer-report of assault aggression and a combined index called 'overall other-report aggression sum'. Combining boys and girls from both junior and senior high schools yielded a positive correlation between these aggression measures and television viewing.

Unfortunately, this finding is an artifact due to the failure to control for the confounding variables of sex and school placement (which related to age) which might be expected to correlate both with aggression and television viewing habits. When the four groups formed by subdividing the sample on the basis of sex and level of high school placement are considered, there remains only one correlation coefficient out of eight which approaches significance! This might be expected by chance alone. For this reason it would be unwise to suggest that the original findings reflect a causal relationship between viewing and aggression.

Similar remarks would apply to the correlations obtained between the amount of violent television viewing and the same measures of aggressive behaviour. The partialled correlation coefficient which reaches marginal significance here completely negates the hypothesis that there is a causal relationship between aggression and violence viewing!

Karp[10] studied the relationship between teacher-ratings of aggression and television viewing in closely matched samples, and supporting the trend of our analysis, found no relationship betwen aggression and television viewing.

The evidence from studies of the relationship betwen television exposure and delinquency is somewhat more clear-cut and reliable as the researchers seem to have been more diligent in controlling for such variables as sex and social class which one would expect to be related to delinquency and television viewing. Halloran, Brown and Chaney[11] explored the television viewing behaviour of probationers and a matched sample of controls. Matching was carried out in terms of age, socio-economic status, sex, intelligence, and school attainment but, of course, there remained factors, such as number of siblings and whether the mother was employed, which could not be controlled. The matching was far better than in many other studies and the study can be seen as comparatively successful in this respect. The research was actually conceived in the context of a uses and gratifications approach to the media and the emphasis was mainly on whether probationers differed from the controls in their television usage. The bulk of the study, then, deals with the reasons probationers gave for liking certain programmes, but figures for the amount of viewing are also presented. There were no significant differences between the probationer sample and the control sample in terms of the number of clock hours during which some television was viewed on weekdays, Saturdays, Sundays, and throughout the week. There were also no differences in the amount of time viewed per evening, the number of evenings spent viewing each week, and the total hours of viewing per week. For this British sample, then, actual exposure to television did not have any relationship to being a probationer. The study collected a certain amount of data on the preferences for different sorts of programmes. Although the authors claim that delinquents tend to prefer 'exciting' programmes (i.e. science fiction, mystery, police, crime, Westerns, spy, thrillers, etc.) which would include the violent programmes which have concerned other researchers, it is difficult to evaluate this finding because proper estimates of sampling error were not calculated and actual measures of exposure to such programmes not made. Certainly the probationers themselves did not seem to regard excitement as an essential component of ideal television programmes. The value of the study for our purposes lies in the exposure variables which are our preferred sort of measure in any case. A study by Bassett, Cowden, and Cohen has yielded similar negative results.[12]

Pfuhl[13] has presented evidence which he adamantly asserts offers no cause for suspicion that television and the other mass media might be implicated in delinquency — any significant correlations being explicable by chance. To some extent this is warranted, but others have pointed to other interpretations of the same data.[14] Things are pretty clear as regards television, however. The subjects of the study were roughly eight hundred boys and girls of 15 — 18 years of age who replied to Pfuhl's questionnaire in conditions of anonymity — an important factor, given that the questions included some concerning delinquency such as purposely damaging or destroying public or private property which did not belong to them. Interpersonal aggression was not measured in this study. The media questions ranged widely and included radio, comic books, and films as well as television. The findings for television indicate that it cannot be implicated in delinquent behaviour. Such diverse measures as time spent watching television, favourite type of television programme, and exposure to television crime dramas did not differentiate delinquents from non-delinquents.

McIntyre and Teevan[15] contributed a fairly massive study of the relationship between media violence and delinquency to the Surgeon General's report on the effects of television violence. They took a sample of over 2,000 white and black, male and female adolescents whom they asked about their television viewing habits and delinquent activities, although they avoided questions about sexual behaviour, drugs, and the more serious types of delinquency because, naturally, the schools were not keen on such data being collected. Delinquency was measured in several ways. Aggressive delinquency was measured using such self-report items as getting into a serious fight with a student at school or hurting someone badly enough for him to need bandages. Petty delinquency was measured by such things as going on to someone's land, or into a house or building when they weren't supposed to, or damaging school property on purpose. Defiance of parents was measured by such things as staying out later than parents said and drinking beer or liquor without parents' permission. The researchers even included a measure of political deviance such as participation in a sit-in or demonstration. The most important sort of deviancy — involvement with legal agencies — was tapped by asking the young people such questions as whether they had been picked up and taken down to the police station or whether they had been brought to the juvenile court.

There were a number of fairly predictable findings about the distributions of these various sorts of deviant behaviour. Boys were found to be in general rather more deviant than girls; and blacks and lower class individuals contribute more than their fair share to the deviancy figures. Obviously such tendencies would alert the researcher to the need to check for possible artifacts due to this.

Television exposure was measured by asking the child to nominate the programmes that he tried to watch every time they were broadcast. These were coded on the basis of their violence content using the categorisations of various adults. Two violence scores were thereby calculated — violence of favourite programme and violence of favourite *four* programmes — and these were computed against measures of delinquency. Only the amount of serious deviancy correlated significantly with the violence rating of the favourite programme, whereas aggressive and serious deviancy correlated with the violence rating of the adolescents' *four* favourite television programmes. While this gives some support for the assertion relating television violence with deviancy, it must be stressed that the degree of association was very small and far from complete. However, the lesson that we have already learned about the effects of confounding variables in such studies needs to be applied here before we can reach any firm conclusions about the effects of media violence. As already suggested, there were indications that deviancy was not evenly distributed through the strata of society, through sex groups, and through races. There were signs that similar factors affect television viewing habits. McIntyre and Teevan state that controlling gender, race, social class and age did not strengthen the relationship between exposure and deviancy. *In fact the associations became smaller and insignificant after partialling out these variables.* There was one trivial exception in that for younger adolescents the correlation remained significant for the serious deviancy measure, but even this could readily be explained on the basis of chance, in view of the many comparisons that were made. Certainly it would be essential to perform multiple partial correlations to investigate the possibility that further confounding variables could explain this finding.

There is nothing in McIntyre and Teevan's data to indicate a strong and reliable relationship between TV exposure and deviancy. Since we can assume that exposure to TV violence does not *cause* age, gender, and so forth, we would be reluctant to accept that these confounding variables in fact are essential links between exposure and delinquency in a causal sequence. McIntyre and Teevan considered other variables which might be expected to facilitate or inhibit the effects of TV violence such as educational expectations, grades in school, integration into school activities, and relationships with parents and peers but these, in fact, did not appear to play a role in the relationship between television violence and deviancy.

At face value one would think that crime statistics would seem a useful dependent variable for the study of media effects, but things are not so straightforward as they might appear. Clearly, if one could find a correlation between the amount of aggression in television programmes and the amount of violent crime in society, one would suspect that television is a likely cause of the violent crime even though conclusive proof is impossible. Since the media are supposed to influence the audience to imitate their aggressive content, a correlation between the violent content of the media and violence in real life would be expected to be found within a few months of changes in media content. There is research available on this point.

However, let us point to the reasons for caution. First of all, it should be noted that official crime statistics refer to crimes reported by or to the police and not necessarily to the actual amount of crime committed. Secondly, since it is reports and not actual frequency of crime, which are reflected by crime statistics, one needs to look for factors determining reporting of crime which might affect these figures. Political 'law and order' campaigns might be expected to increase the diligence of the police in searching for crimes, to increase the police's encouragement of individuals to press their complaints, and to encourage the police to press for convictions on the more serious charges. Not only would such campaigns encourage police action but the general public might be more willing to report crimes and expect police action, following such changes in the 'moral' climate. Clearly, since there are so many confounding factors in crime statistics, they form a better index of reporting activity than they do of criminal activity. One can expect that there would be less effect of these confounding factors on crimes (such as murder) which are detected and reported in almost every instance than on crimes which may go unnoticed or unreported. For this reason murder rates (despite problems of changing definitions of murder) would be a better index of change than crimes less frequently reported. For example, crimes of aggravated assault, according to U.S. uniform crime reports, seem to have at least doubled per 100,000 population between 1933 and 1968, but the rate of murders has remained remarkably constant during this same period — this despite the introduction of television during this time. For such reasons one would be disinclined to use violent crime statistics in reaching conclusions about the effects of TV violence. However, since these self-same figures have been used to hint that we are becoming a more and more violent society, it is not unreasonable to assess the link between real life violence and television violence on the self-same basis, even though scientifically we would wish to take a much more conservative stand.[16]

Clark and Blankenburg[17] studied the relationship between the crime statistics and the violence content of television. They used the TV programme magazine *TV Guide* as a basis for their assessment of the violent content of television for each of the years 1953-69. This American magazine contains synopses of the content of each of the programmes, from which it is possible to evaluate roughly their violent content. Coders were asked to indicate whether each of the synopses contained a significant indication of physical violence in the programme content. There is considerable fluctuation in the amount of violence shown over the years. Clark and Blankenburg suggest that the violence content of television is cyclical, reaching peaks roughly every four years. They found no relationship between the violent content of a year's television programming and the crime figures for that year. Further, there was no significant correlation between a year's television violent content and the crime statistics of the following year. This is important because it suggests that the lack of correlation of each year's crime figures with each year's violent fictional content cannot be explained away by the assumption that it would take a little while for the effects of mass media violence to filter through society and into the crime statistics.

These findings certainly indicate that crime statistics are uninfluenced by violent TV content, but whether they tell us anything about the real rates of crime in society is a different matter. In the sixth chapter we discuss further findings of this study which indicate that violent TV content can be influenced by various social factors, but this need not concern us here. Finally, Himmelweit, Openheim and Vince[18] could find no differences between television viewers and non-viewers in terms of teacher ratings of aggression. Menzies[19] could find no evidence that assaultive prisoners differed from controls in preferences for violent television; and Mills[20] could find no relevant differences in the television habits of aggressive and non-aggressive twelve year olds!

In summary, there is no reliable evidence that television exposure, whether general or violent, has any causal relationship with relevant dependent variables such as aggression or delinquency. A number of studies which at face value indicate a relationship can be seen to be flawed in that controls for essential variables such as sex are neglected. This failure confounds a relationship which becomes insignificant when appropriate controls are made.

CINEMA

While those critical of the media have tended to be unselective as to which they blame for crime and violence, this view is not supported by the data. Whereas the television studies reviewed above reveal no relationship

106

between television viewing and either aggression or delinquency when statistical artifacts are dealt with, there is a fairly consistent relationship found between cinema and aggression or delinquency as the following review shows.

Pfuhl's[21] study revealed this difference between the media very effectively. For boys there was a significant relationship between frequency of attendance at motion pictures and delinquency and between the number of crime movies seen recently and delinquency. For girls, delinquency was associated only with high frequency of cinema attendance and not with the number of crime movies seen. The favourite sorts of film did not differentiate delinquents from non-delinquents whether male or females are considered.

Shuttleworth and May[22] in their contribution to the Payne Fund studies of the early 1930s, compared those children attending the cinema frequently with those not attending so frequently. Movie attenders have 'average lower deportment records, do on the average poorer work in their school subjects, are rated lower in reputation by their teachers on two rating forms, are rated lower by their classmates on the Guess Who test, are less cooperative and less self-controlled as measured both by ratings and conduct tests, are slightly more deceptive in school situations, slightly less skilful in judging what is the most useful and helpful and sensible thing to do, and are somewhat less emotionally stable'. Interestingly, and this is important in our interpretation of the data, the heavy movie attender is more popular than the low attender.

Another study contributed to the Payne Fund series suggested a strong relationship between the movies and delinquency. Cressey and Thrasher[23] noted that delinquents and truants tend more often than others to go excessively to the cinema. Healy and Bronner[24] also found that delinquents attend the cinema more frequently than non-delinquents.

The only study not showing such a relationship is that of Karp[25] who found that non-aggressive boys tended to visit the cinema significantly more frequently than aggressive boys. This finding does not appear to be artifactual, but it is worthwile noting that the aggressive and non-aggressive samples consist of only twenty-six individuals. On the other hand, there was evidence that the aggressive boys had a greater interest in war films.

This one study aside, the question of the effects of uncontrolled variables on this relationship deserves some attention. The obvious variable, other than sex which was controlled in Pfuhl's study and so need not concern us, is social class. It might be expected that delinquency is associated with social class and it is possible that cinema attendance is correlated with this variable. The best evidence on this comes again from Pfuhl who found that although class differences correlated with the attendance differences for boys, social class differences were not associated with his measure of delinquency.[26] Thus the class variable is unimportant as an explanation of the cinema/delinquency relationship. Further, since for girls social class neither correlated with cinema attendance nor delinquency, the possibility of such a confounding variable as class explaining the relationship is even less likely.

Since all but one of the studies mentioned here have demonstrated a strong relationship between the cinema and various sorts of delinquent behaviour, we have firm ground for assuming the validity of the assertion connecting delinquency with cinema attendance. However, we will have to make the reservation, at this point, that aggression *per se* has not been shown to bear a strong relationship with cinema exposure. This is simply because of the absence of relevant studies.

RADIO

There is absolutely no evidence that listening to radio is associated with aggression or delinquency. In fact for some reason there seems to be little public concern about the issue, as far as can be judged from the research effort directed at the medium. Pfuhl[27] found no differences in delinquency related to time spent listening to the radio, favourite type of radio show, and regular exposure to radio crime dramas. Ricuitti[28] found no evidence of a relationship, although he used only projective measures of undesirable behaviour. The limited evidence leads to an assumption of no relationship but one would like to see a wider range of studies related to the radio, particularly since the above studies were carried out before the boom in the sales of transistor radios brought about radical changes in the uses and functions of the medium.[29]

COMIC BOOKS

Comic books, unlike the radio, have often been accused of having undesirable effects. Action against comic books has been more extreme than for most other media as far as the control of their content is concerned.[30] There has correspondingly been more attention paid to comic books as a cause of delinquency.

Hoult[31] carried out the most frequently cited study in this area. He took a sample of boys and girls arrested for delinquency ranging from ten to seventeen years of age and matched these with a non-delinquent group on the basis of sex, age, school level, and socioeconomic status. Quite what the matching on social class was is unclear from Hoult's report and, in fact, he suggests that he only matched 'generally speaking' for socioeconomic status. This leaves open the possibility of an artifact due to class. Hoult's findings were that:

The delinquents reported that they read a total of 2,853 'harmful' and 'questionable' comic books, while the non-delinquents reported that they read only 1,786 of the same types. Although both groups chose 'Crime does not pay' as their favorite 'comic' the delinquents read many more of the crime, the 'blood and thunder', and the supernatural action books. The delinquents read 762 of the crime books, whereas the non-delinquents read considerably fewer, with a total of 491. While the delinquents calimed that they read 331 'blood and thunder' books regularly, the non-delinquents said that they read only 153 of this variety.

Although Hoult does not specify exactly what the classifications meant, there is little reason to doubt that his findings reveal a strong association between comic book reading and delinquency.

These findings have not been completely paralleled in the conclusions of other researchers. Pfuhl[32] had several different measures of exposure to crime and similar comics. His indexes included time spent reading comic magazines, exposure to horror comics, and exposure to crime comics. Only one of these variables was significantly associated with delinquency — and that for girls. It was found that delinquent girls were exposed to crime comics more often than non-delinquent girls. Karp[33] could detect no differences between aggressive and non-aggressive boys in terms of their frequencies of comic book readership, their frequency of crime comic book readership, and their favourite comic book content (violence versus non-violence). Lewin[34] has shown that for 12 and 13 year old boys comic book readership seems to have no impact on delinquency, truancy, and performance and conduct in school.

The relationship between comics and delinquency is less clear-cut than that for the other media. It is difficult to draw threads which integrate the various studies.

OTHER MEDIA

Media such as the newspapers and books are not often implicated in the debate about the undesirable effects of the media on young people. Of course, the obscenity debate is to some extent an exception — at least as far as books are concerned. The available research suggests little cause for concern. Healy and Bonner[35] found that the delinquents tended to be more fond of reading and read with greater breadth than their non-delinquents! Additionally, Karp's[36] aggressive boys tended to read more books than the non-aggressive sample.

Pfuhl[37] found no significant differences in the number of crime and mystery novels read by high and low delinquents although there was some very slight evidence that the delinquent boys had a greater interest in crime and mystery novels. Whatever these relationships mean, it is clear that a simple causal explanation is not really on the cards. In Karp's study, there was no difference between the aggressive and non-aggressive boys in terms of newspaper exposure.

This review of the literature suggests a number of conclusions which might validly be drawn:

1. Correlational research has tended to give a very equivocal answer

to the question of the relationship between both delinquency and aggression and the mass media. Because of this no single assertion about the dangers of the mass media portrayal of violence can be made.

2. Not all of the media of mass communication seem equally associated with aggression and delinquency. There is, for example, very little sound evidence which asserts a positive relationship between television exposure and delinquency or aggression, while there is a good deal of evidence asserting a strong correlation between such variables and motion picture habits. A simple model of social learning from media content could not really account for these findings since one would expect, because the cinema and television both tend to be violent, that the relationship between socialisation found for one would apply to the other.

This data may, at first sight, seem confusing, but integrating accounts have been put forward which do not rely on a simplistic model of media effect.

Theory indicates that the best way of looking at this data is not in terms of the effect of the media in socialising children into crime and violence, but in terms of the differential use to which the media are put. This is, as might be expected, in line with the 'uses and gratifications' approach to media research which has often been propounded but differs in that the uses described are not really 'psychological needs' such as affiliation, excitement, and the like but merely utilitarian habits of certain sorts of young people. This will become clearer as the model is expanded.

THE SUBCULTURAL ACCOUNT OF
MEDIA-VIOLENCE-DELINQUENCY RELATIONSHIP

Every medium can serve functions over and above its manifest content. Newspapers ostensibly teach us about news but are often used to while away time on the train to work, for example. Television can be used as a conversation piece as well as a source of entertainment, and so forth. The account of the media-violence-delinquency relationships proposed here depends for its explanatory power precisely on this sort of secondary function. Most particularly it is the use which delinquent subcultures will make of the cinema which forms the basis of our model.

It is common experience that the cinema is not just a place of entertainment. It tends to be a meeting point for young people, some of which are members of adolescent groups — the very groups which one would expect to be involved in delinquent activities. One would not suggest that all of these young people are in some way delinquent but the tendency would be for these youngster to be more delinquent than the young people who stayed at home. There is nothing very profound about this point but it does go a long way to understanding the violence/delinquency relationship with the cinema. Of course, not all cinemas can be regarded as social meeting grounds for young people — it is the less expensive and less particular cinema that would tend to attract this sort of clientele. Actual sociological study of the phenomenon has been very infrequent even though most of us have had some experience of it. The only study systematically exploring cinema behaviour in young people was carried out as part of the Payne Fund series and deserves considerable attention. R.L. Whitley, the senior researcher on the team before he died, with the research incomplete, wrote:

In a number of cases the motion picture house is much more important in relation to delinquency than is the material shown on the screen. The motion picture house is generally dimly lighted. Ordinarily there are some sections of the house where few people are sitting. The house in general is one of the most convenient spots in the community, for these reasons, in which boys may engage in a variety of sexual practices; especially during daylight, there are few spots in the community where boys may engage in sexual practices with girls without being apprehended and punished. Occasionally the boy is able to find a vacant or secluded spot in the park, but ordinarily he confines his sexual activities outside the movie house to the night. As a consequence a variety of sexual practices are observed by the boy ordinarily in the movie house, and occasionally he engages in various forms of sex activity in the the house itself.[38]

This passage conjures up ideas of debauchery at the Roxy, but it is quoted since it demonstrates vividly that the motion picture theatre can be seen to have less direct functions than simply screening films.[39] Although Whitley scarcely took a representative sample of motion picture theatres on which to form his perspective, there can be little doubt that there is a good deal of generality in his assertions. On this assumption that cinemas function as meeting places for young people, some of whom will engage in delinquent activity, it might be suggested that we need look no further for reasons why aggression and delinquency correlate with motion picture attendance. The reason is clear — it is not the content of the medium which socialises the child into delinquency but that delinquency prone children are likely to visit the cinema more than the more normal child.

Television is, in this light, a radically different sort of medium. Rather than taking the child out of the home it is an activity largely confined to the home. The child for whom his peers are important would scarcely be expected to watch television to excess — his taste would be to be out and about with his friends. If the subcultural theory is correct, one would not expect that television exposure and aggression or delinquency correlate positively. If anything, one would expect that there would be a slight negative correlation. As our review of the literature showed, television exposure does not correlate significantly with aggression and delinquency, a finding which is perfectly in line with the subcultural model. There is one question, however, which might cause some worry here. That is, if the delinquent child prefers activities not centred around the home, would we not expect a strong negative correlation between television exposure and aggression or delinquency? Eron's study alone showed this, while most studies have found neither a positive nor a negative relationship. There are many reasons why this might be so. We do not know the precise exposure habits of the aggressive and delinquent child. Perhaps he watches television at rather different times of the day to the non-delinquent or non-aggressive child. There is evidence that this is so.[40] In addition cinema attendance takes up little time compared to that which young people devote to television and, given the lack of reliability of measures of television exposure, one would not expect the television measures to be as discriminating as those for the cinema.

Basically the argument is that the manifest content of the medium cannot explain the relation between cinema attendance and delinquency. This seems obvious once it has been expressed but it has essentially eluded researchers over the last half century. It is in a sense too easy to assume the social equivalence of all of the different sorts of media — not that we have been unaware of the different sorts of audiences for the different media. The cinema, for example, has always tended to have predominantly young audiences which would suggest that it functions to satisfy the needs of younger people rather than those of older people.[41]

The weakness of our argument up to this point is that it is based on a wide variety of different studies which deal with aggression and delinquency, but we have presented no systematic evidence on the social behaviour of these types of youths which is relevant to our argument. Perhaps the ideal study would attempt to show that aggressive and delinquent boys were different from controls in the extent to which they are integrated in peer group culture. If it could be shown (for the critical instance of the cinema) that the peer group integration is a better predictor of media exposure than aggression, and if it could further be shown that aggression without the peer integration factor is a very poor predictor of media use, one would be fully justified in claiming that exposure to the mass media does not cause aggression but rather that aggression (due to its association with peer group integration) causes exposure to the mass media.

A second weakness of the argument is its inability to explain the relationship between aggression or delinquency and exposure to comic books. The available studies are far from being unequivocal on what the relationship actually is. Hoult's study is perhaps the strongest evidence for the hypothesis but other studies (e.g. that of Pfuhl) paint a less positive picture. Howitt[42] asserted that comic books might be expected to have this functional relevance to peer groups because they were readily transportable — a sort of currency which could be passed from hand to hand by young people. One way of beginning to integrate these disparate findings would be to suggest that the cultural meaning of comic books changed with the public uproar following the campaigns of the 1950s which culminated in fairly radical revisions of the content of comic books. Since, once the medium is divorced from its undesirable content its interest for the peer group orientated child is diminished, the relationship between comic book reading and delinquency or aggression should have changed with the passage of time. Unfortunately the data is not clear enough to assert anything strongly about this, but it is notable that recent studies have tended to discount such a relationship.

Empirical support for the subcultural notion of media and violence/aggression relationships can be gleaned from the work of Richard Dembo.[43] This study is probably the best of those dealing correlationally with the question of media impact. It was painstaking in its attempts to achieve measures of aggression and self-image which were related to the actual life experiences of young people rather than being merely the whims of the researcher. Stringent efforts were made to control for extraneous variables such as class and age which have tended to confound the results of many other studies. Further, the study is exceptional in that it deals with a full range of media rather than concentrating on just a single medium in isolation. Eight media were covered in detail including books, cinema, comics, magazines, newspapers, radio, records and television. The final sample contained only ninety-nine adolescent boys but the careful interviewing and piloting work involved encourage us to generalise from this modest sample. The research will be described in detail so that the reader can appreciate its thoroughness.

During the course of exploratory field work at a youth club servicing a large council estate, Dembo collected a series of recordings of group discussion concerning working class boys' perceptions of what is aggressive. One of the things to emerge in the discussion was that the boys maintained a distinction between what they term 'hard guys' and the others (which we may call non-hard guys although no doubt the boys had more explicit language). This notion of 'hard guy' is roughly equated with aggression, as can be seen by the fact that the hard guy would tend to be cheeky and answer teachers back, tend to violate school rules, start fights with others to preserve his aggressive reputation, and use his fists to achieve his ends. These indicators of aggression were rather different to those used by most researchers in that they are to do with violence rather than a more general conception of assertiveness. Dembo used these characteristics of the 'hard guy' as the basis of scales for peer ratings of aggression.

Each boy rated himself and his class-mates on being cheeky to teacher, being disobedient of rules, being aggressive for status, and using his fists to achieve his ends. The rating procedure was completely blind, the researcher who collected the aggression data taking no part in the later interviews, to avoid biases during the interview. These measures seem to have good validity when compared with teacher assessments made on the same variables and enabled two groups of boys — high and low peer rated aggressives — to be selected.

During the interview proper, two measures were taken which are of importance to our argument. *Street Culture Orientation* was a measure of the boy's acceptance of the values of the outward looking, clannish adolescent teenage group with the emphasis on toughness, leadership, and sexual prowess. The items took the form of brief cameos to which the boy had to say whether they described him or not. They included: *'Charlie* is never stuck for things to do or places to go. He is a natural leader and the rest of the group usually follow him' and *'Jason* is a hard guy and enjoys proving how really tough he is. He is the kind of guy you can depend on in a fight.' The other important self-perception measure, *Toughness Orientation*, consisted of such items as 'You've got to be tough to get on around here' and 'People of my age in my neighbourhood get into fights.'

Of course, as might be expected, *Peer Rated Aggression* correlated with both *Street Culture Orientation* and *Toughness Orientation*. However, they are not the same thing. Unlike the other two, *Street Culture Orientation* is not primarily concerned with aggression or toughness (although it does correlate with them) but with the values of the street culture. The difference is highlighted by the pattern of media use. *Peer Rated Aggression* and *Toughness Orientation* did not correlate with media exposure. There was no tendency, then, for toughness orientated and aggressive youngsters to use any of the mass media more than the youngsters low on these traits. All in all there is no support in this data for the fears of the effects of the mass media on aggressive behaviour.

Although this data does not support the violence amplification model of the effects of the mass media, there is also so far no direct support for our sub-cultural explanation of previous research. Since our subcultural model postulates that the differential use of the media by delinquent boys is not due to the socialisation influences of the media content but due to an artifact caused by the failure to understand the different social utilitarian functions of the different media, this data is not necessarily an embarrassment to our position. Fortunately, *Street Culture Orientation* provides the evidence we need.

114

Street Culture Orientation measures commitment to some of the adolescent cultural values outside of the home and school. Its focus is the peer group values of adolescent youth. It is this very measure which forms the critical test of the subcultural hypothesis — not the measures of aggression and toughness pure and simple. In a sense, the model argues that aggression will only correlate with media exposure to the extent that it is related to peer group membership and especially to street cultures. We have already pointed out that *Street Culture Orientation* contains this essential aggressive element and that, despite this, the two things are to a large extent independent. The raw correlations of *Street Culture Orientation* with media exposure measures support the hypothesis reasonably well. Of the eight different media exposure patterns studied, only two were significantly associated with *Street Culture Orientation.* These were cinema attendance and time spent listening to records. While our model has little to say about records, the cinema attendance finding is directly in line with our integration of the previous studies described above. Records can readily be seen to have a similar sort of social utilitarian function to that of the cinema. It has been documented by researchers that popular youths tend to be more highly orientated to popular music output than the less popular ones.[44] These results clearly show that it is peer group orientation rather than aggression *per se* which determines media exposure, although we know that *Street Culture Orientation* does include a component of aggression.

Basically, then, Dembo's data increases more than somewhat our confidence in the subcultural account of media and delinquency/violence relationships. There is in all the studies reviewed no more than a modicum of evidence which does not fit the account we have offered. Even the little evidence that does not fit perfectly far from indicates the reverse of our assertions and consists of evidence of a null relationship rather than a significant reversal of our account. The interpretation on which we base our discussion is not quite in line with what the original author had concluded in every case (this is especially true of some of the Surgeon General Reports) and the reader is warned not to assume that our discussion concurs with that of the original researcher.

The interesting thing about this model, leaving aside its explanatory power, is that it implies almost that the medium is the message and that it is not the manifest content of the thematic material intrinsic to the medium that causes effects. The question of why the media do not seem to have the effects commonly ascribed to them remains to be investigated, but it is reasonable to conclude that emphasis on media effects is a fruitless occupation as far as aggression is concerned. The evidence presented in this chapter constitutes quite a powerful argument against searching in the mass media for answers to the question of the causes of aggression and delinquency. Although, as has often been pointed out, no one asserts that the mass media cause all violence and delinquency — the common assumption being that only a minute fraction of violence and delinquency can be attributed to the viewing of television and exposure to other mass media, nevertheless a considerable amount of public money has been contributed to research in this area. One would not wish to imply that this money has been wasted — that we are coming to some sort of evaluation based on this research argues against this — but only that public concern with the mass media has tended to limit itself too readily to the areas of effects without considering more precisely the role of the mass media in society.[45]

This and the previous two chapters have shown effectively that the mass media — as far as it is possible to tell using social scientific methodologies — do not serve to amplify the level of violence in society. However, this is far from being the ultimate concern that one could express about television and other mass media violence. The final chapter gives an account of some of these further causes for concern and sets out the general conclusions of this work.

CHAPTER SIX
SOME FURTHER
CONSIDERATIONS

In this book we have been concerned with evaluating the main body of social scientific research relevant to the public debate on the effects of mass media violence. The central theme of this research is the evaluation of the effects of media violence on the willingness of an individual to behave aggressively. However, the problem of media violence is broader than this and we will now turn to some other considerations which go some way towards tempering the *carte blanche* which our discussion has so far offered the mass media. Just because it is doubtful that the media contribute significantly to the level of violence in society does not absolve them in any way from responsibilities in other directions. The questions of the impact of violence on programming and programme quality, the distress caused to young viewers, and the affront to the sensibilities of a minority all need careful attention. In this final chapter we will review some of the reasons why a wider perspective on media violence as a social concern is needed. In addition, we appreciate that because our view is so contrary to the popular one, it is possible that some readers may still entertain some reservations about our conclusions. We hope that the closing remarks of this book will anticipate and partially answer some of the remaining questions.

WHAT CAN PARENTS DO ABOUT MEDIA VIOLENCE?

Parents concerned about the effects of media violence on their children may not be too convinced by our assertion that the media have no effect and press the question 'What can I do to protect my child from the influence of mass media violence?' Erring on the side of caution may be old fashioned but it is nevertheless a virtue. Let us assume for a moment that we had concluded on the basis of the available evidence that the mass media *do* cause the child viewer to become more aggressive towards others in society, that they cause delinquency, and that the child needs protection from the influence of the mass media. How then could the parent fight the media monster?

The notion that the parent can shield the child from the harsh brutality of the television screen is frequently expressed. Frailberg has written, for example:

. . . we must reflect upon our position as moral educators when we teach our children to renounce sadism, and destructive tendencies within themselves, at the same time that we hold daily open house to the underworld of television, its gangsters, extortionists, and assorted ghouls in the family living room. It has always been the prerogative of parents to exclude unwelcome influences from the home, to declare their opposition to alien and hostile forces by not keeping company with them. This is not to say that one pretended they did not exist, which is an absurd position for a parent, but to make explicit the moral stand of the family through a gesture of inhospitality or exclusion. During the years that a child must learn his parents' stand on a variety of moral issues, it is undoubtedly a help to him to know which ideas are given hospitality in his home and which are not. But how is he to make sense out of an ambiguous parental stand which deplores and abhors on the one hand and permits and entertains on the other?[1]

The freedom to switch off has considerable appeal though it is of little relevance to diffuse households where many different individuals have control of the television set. The other possibility — that television violence should be regarded almost as if it provided a case study for the discussion or moral principles — seems somewhat unrealistic. Empirical evidence in favour of parental intervention of one sort or another in the child's media consumption is scant. Although it would come as no surprise to mass communication researchers if it were found that the primary social group has a profound mediating effect on the relationship between television exposure and aggression, direct evidence of this has not been forthcoming.[2] There is a rather simple-minded study in the literature which suggests that imitation of a model may be inhibited by the experimenter instructing the child not to copy the modelled behaviour,[3] but this would not be a good foundation for the parent's policy towards media violence.

Perhaps the most relevant and useful studies here are those of McLeod and Chaffee[4] who investigated the effects of parental control over and the interpretation of mass media violence on the behaviour of their children. Parental control over television was tapped by asking the child 'Who has most to say about what you watch on television?', 'Do your parents always know what programmes you are watching on TV?', 'Are there certain programmes that your parents sometimes do not let you watch?', and 'When you watched action-adventure shows with your parents, how often did they used to say these things if someone in the story was hurt badly, during westerns and crime shows? — Told you that things are not like this in real life? Said that these stories are "just pretend". Explained that there are better ways than violence to solve problems. Said you shouldn't do the bad things people do on TV, and reminded you that the people on TV are just actors and not really getting hurt?'

An interesting point which emerged was that it tended to be the child and not the parent who took the lead in determining what programmes the family watched. However, the question of who decides the type of programmes the different members of the family watch is not of primary importance. What is central is that the families in which attempts were made to control the adolescent's television viewing and to interpret the violent content of television were not very effective in decreasing television violence viewing. In fact, viewing was higher in the children of such families than those in which efforts at control were not made! McLeod and Chaffee suggest that this is because those families which attempted to control the child were doing so because they were aware that their children watched too much television and were trying to modify its influence. Another interpretation might be that attempts to control the behaviour of adolescents simply increase the desirability of the sanctioned behaviour. That is, perhaps the children watch these programmes simply because the parents do not wish them to.

There was no tendency for parental controls and explanations to increase or reduce the relationship between television viewing and aggressive behaviour. In fact there was no correlation between the parental intervention measures with respect to the mass media and the child's aggressive behaviour. This would be fully expected on the basis of our account of the media effects studies, but difficult to reconcile with the view that the mass media help to cause the level of violence in society. McLeod and Chaffee are not as unhelpful to the parent as this account would imply. They write:

> The control over viewing is really an indirect parental strategy, attempting to ultimately limit or reduce aggression by first limiting the child's intake of media violence. Our data suggest a more direct strategy of emphasizing non-aggression to the child. This entails telling the child not to fight back if other kids pick on him, warning him not to imitate aggressive acts seen on television, and so forth. While this emphasis will not appeal to many parents, our findings indicate that it operates as a strong contingent variable reducing the violence viewing-aggressive behaviour correlation markedly.

> The parent might also consider using restraint in the application of punishment. While most parents seem to realise the negative effects of physical punishment, the potential dangers of verbal and restrictive punishments are less well recognised. In particular, our data indicate that restrictive punishment ('grounding' and taking away privileges) is linked to viewing and aggression.[5]

Clearly there can be little objection to the assertion that the best way to avoid aggression in children is to concentrate on the aggressive behaviour itself rather than the effects of television viewing. Stop people aggressing and violent television cannot be a cause for concern. This is, of course, to take a rather atheoretical view of our knowledge. Although it is perfectly reasonable to argue that the social structure through which the media permeate explains their lack of effects, it would be wrong to assume that the role of the social environment with respect to aggression is simply to modify the influence of the mass media (there is evidence against this supposition in the research of McIntyre and Teevan[6]). Social influences socialise children independently of the mass media. It is a trivial point, but we all know that people were violent before there were mass media. Since violence is an established fact of life in the absence of the mass media, only a portion, at best, of violence could be controlled by controlling media content.

This leads to another important question — that of the influence of other agents of socialisation such as the church and school on inhibiting the (presumed) effects of mass media violence on children. It would not be surprising that those children who were effectively socialised by such organisations would be buffered against the 'subversive' influence of the mass media. In a sense this is merely an extension of the dictum that one cannot understand violence in the mass media unless one understands the role of and controls of violence in society. Certainly it would be reasonable to assume that this immunity provided by a strong moral environment would reduce the influence of the media on children. This is not far removed from the reinforcement notion of the effects of mass media commonly accepted by those who have studied communication effectiveness. A distinct question is whether the child's aggressive behaviour is so well socialised that the mass media could not possibly have an effect. That is, are the children who are not socialised by the church and family to a firmly anti-violence code of conduct completely unsocialised on violence? They could have learned their lessons for good or bad by other means. This second position would mean that the moral institutions in society might not necessarily have any influence at all on the (assumed) relationship between mass media exposure and violence in the young audience.

McIntyre and Teevan[7] provided evidence relevant to this issue in their study of the relationship between mass media violence and deviancy. They term these moral forces 'insulating factors' and ask the question 'whether such ties to the social structure mediate between television violence and aggressive deviance?' predicting that 'weaker and fewer insulating ties to the social structure will strengthen the relationship between television and deviance'. Their insulating factors were expectations of educational success, aspirations to high level occupations, expectations of or actual achieved job position, participation in school activities, relationship with peers, and fear of punishment which were combined to form an index of insulation from

120

the effects of the mass media. While the measure seems, at face value, to have considerable validity in that the adolescents with few insulating factors tend to have high aggressive deviance scores, the data suggest no greater relationship between violence in the media and violence in real life for those low in insulating factors than for those high in insulating factors.

The evidence as it stands, even assuming the effects of mass media violence on real life violence, indicates that no matter what the parent might attempt to do to shield the child from the undesirable socialising influence of television, the efforts are doomed to failure. This is hardly surprising if the mass media have no effect on the level of real life violence. This is, not of course, to say that moral institutions are not of primary importance in the socialisation process, but only that they are irrelevant to the issue of mass media violence. A note of caution should be sounded in that the available research deals with adolescents and not with very young children. Possibly the effects are not the same for all age groups.

DISTRESS AND ANXIETY

There is little doubt that mass media portrayals of violence can cause distress and anxiety in the audience. However, whether this is a good or bad thing is uncertain. It is difficult to conceive that one would wish to protect the public forever from the horrors of war, armed conflict, aggression and the like, but it is also true that one would not wish the audience to be assaulted simply 'for kicks'. The question must be one of balance involving various incompletely specifiable factors related to the justifiability of different sorts of events. What might on occasion be appropriate for a late night documentary on civil unrest might not be appropriate for common or garden children's television programmes. Such questions of the propriety of violent episodes are not the domain of social scientific research. However, evidence on which types of programmes cause distress or anxiety is readily tackled by the methods of social research.

Lyle and Hoffmann[8] asked a sample of American children if they had ever been scared by the things that they had seen on television. Forty-eight per cent of boys and 31% of girls said that they had *never* been scared by television content whereas 33% of boys and 50% of girls said that they sometimes had been. The *often* and *not very often* categories each accounted for 10% of the cases each. Since the children were six or seven years old perhaps we are dealing with the most vulnerable section of the audience. Interestingly enough, and as might be expected, the programmes which frightened the children were precisely those programmes designed to scare the audience — 88% of the frightening programmes fell into what Lyle and Hoffmann deem the 'chiller/monster' category. However, straightforward shooting and detective type violence was mentioned by 8% of the sample who reported having been scared by things on television.

It is not always the expected content of the mass media which disturbs the young viewer. For example, one study concerned adolescents' response to a film which had been singled out because it contained a fair amount of bad language, although it was far from extreme in this respect.[9] The child audience was far less bothered by this than by the non-violent death of the mother of some of the children in the film. Likewise an audience study of the Andy Warhol film *Trash*[10] revealed that close-ups of injections produced more distress in the audience than masturbation, fellatio, nudity and obscenity.[11]

In the pioneering television research of Himmelweit, Oppenheim and Vince,[12] the question of the factors in television violence causing anxiety and distress was covered in some detail. Programmes which frightened adolescents included 'mystery and horror plays and horrific space fiction programmes' — much the same sort of programme which frightened Lyle and Hoffmann's sample. In summary Himmelweit *et al* suggest several factors which reduce the disturbing aspects of television violence and aggression:

1. The stylisation of violence: The more violence follows the conventions of drama rather than the conventions of real life, the less impact will the violence have.

2. The more unfamiliar the settings of the violence, the less distressing the violence (although this is constrained to the settings which are not eerie or spooky).

3. The more clear-cut the character, the less distressing his aggression. The sharp distinction between goodies and baddies is important here.

4. The events are make-believe rather than realistic.

5. The less children identify with characters, the less they worry about them.

Not all sorts of violence have equivalent impact on the child viewer. For example knives were more disturbing than guns. Young children were more frightened than older children, girls more frightened than boys. As might be expected, the number of people injured or the number of gun shots are relatively unimportant factors.

This is an area where research has not been very forthcoming, partly, one imagines, because of the difficulty of measuring fear and distress adequately and partly due to the lack of clear indications for social policy which lead from such data. If Himmelweit's points about TV violence were applied rigidly they would scarcely lead to many people's ideal programmes.

There are indications that the media institutions are well aware of the subtleties of the child's response to television programmes. In the British Broadcasting Corporation's Code of Practice some of the differences between adults' and childrens' reponses to television are noted, for example:

> The worlds which children and grown-ups occupy, though they overlap, are different. Subjects with unpleasant associations for the one will often be taken for granted by the other. Guns and fisticuffs may have sinister implications for adults; seldom for children. Family insecurity and marital infidelity may be commonplace to adults; to children they can be deeply disturbing.[13]

Clearly this is an area in which there is a great need for research and careful thought about control. If, as seems to be so, what may be an innocuous piece for most viewers disturbs others, this presents awkward questions for social policy. The example of the distress caused to children by media presentations of family insecurity and marital infidelity is a good one in this context. These themes are fairly common in fully admirable dramatic presentations and one would find it undesirable to avoid them altogether even in the early evening periods when children are most likely to be watching. On the other hand, it is clear from research that many children do watch television well after nine o'clock in the evening so, in a sense, the problem remains unsolved. Obviously each case must be considered on its merits — a suggestion which appears more innocuous than it really is.

WHY TELEVISION VIOLENCE?

The effects of vicarious violence, whether on aggression or anxiety, are not the be-all and end-all of the concern about mass media portrayals of violence. Because the mass media, particularly television, are pervasive throughout society and contribute a good deal to the entertainment and leisure of vast proportions of the population, one can scarcely consider that proof of lack of effects is enough to remove all cause for concern over violent television content. Why there is so much violence in mass media programming is equally as valid a research question as what is the effect of mass media violence. Questions of the relationship between the media and the audience, of how the media satisfy public needs, of the extent to which revenues and audience figures determine programme decisions are all implicit in the 'why' question. Whatever the purpose of the mass media, it is clear that their content is of primary interest.

We have several sources of information concerning the reasons for so much violence in the mass media — especially in entertainment programmes. We must not assume, however, that violence is the dominant theme of all mass media. For example using the formal definitions of content analysis, newspapers in general contain relatively little of it. Television cartoons, on the other hand, tend to have the greatest concentration of violence of all television programmes. Television news does have a lot of references to violence, but non-violence dominates. Fictional material tends to contain a preponderence of violent fare — not necessarily violent in the sense of causing profound physical harm to the victim, but physical aggression none the less.

Clark and Blankenburg's[14] study was described in the previous chapter where it was shown that ratings of TV content did not correlate with crime statistics. This was a minor aspect of the study which was predominantly concerned with the factors determinining TV violence. While investigating other correlates of violent television they discovered an interesting association between violence and viewing figures. Although the number of violent shows did not correlate significantly with the ratings of the popularity of the violent programmes for the same year, there was a significant correlation between the popularity of violent programmes one year and the number of violent programmes broadcast during the following year. This lag would seem to suggest that the industry needs time to respond to the outcome of audience research. Filmed series take time to plan and produce. Clark and Blankenburg write in summary of their research:

> Violence on television appears to run in four or five year cycles, and the audience ratings do correlate positively with the percentages of violent programs. As violent types of programs gain popularity, their numbers increase until they become so directly competitive that their ratings are diluted, until the audience tires, or until public and official criticism makes itself heard. Programming officials have long been concerned about the effects criticism might have on them and on their advertising clients. Network machinery has worked to moderate both the form of violence and, to a lesser degree, its extent, for short periods until other factors (chiefly competition) begin to start the new cycle. The audience appears to have a high tolerance — if not affinity — for violence. The wider fluctuations in number of violent type programs than of other kinds suggests that networks regard violence as good bait, while such programs as variety and comedy are basic content and hence less variable in number[15]

This argument basically asserts that violence is used as a tool for attracting audiences and that when audiences tire of violence or when public concern about violence reaches a peak, the amount of violence portrayed on the screen is then dampened. To some extent, then, feedback from the audience (complaints from politicians or decline in public interest) serves to restrict television content and prevent violence from escalating beyond certain limits. While this research originates in the U.S.A., it might be assumed that parallel processes operate elsewhere. Important questions therefore arise as to how these controls are achieved by the media organisations. For example one might be concerned as to how 'censorship' influences the creativity of the writer and the producer of television series, who communicates to the producer that a show needs more or less violence and under what conditions, how the interests of advertisers are accommodated in the television industry's output, and how political and other pressure-group condemnations of violence influence programming. Evidence on the effects of advertising pressures, audience figures and organisational concern with the 'political' ramifications of too much TV violence comes largely from interviews with relevant media personnel, the content of which may reflect irrelevant aspects of the individual's lot such as his own private grouses and frustrations, but this evidence still deserves consideration since it points to some of the difficulties involved in the control of fictional violence. Baldwin and Lewis[16] interviewed a wide range of individuals engaged in the production of television programmes and, as might be expected, found a variety of opinions not necessarily fully compatible with one another. For example, on the question of the drawing power of violence one producer told the researchers:

The audience wants and approves of violence under certain conditions. For instance, in *Bad Day at Black Rock*, Spencer Tracey takes punishment from a guy, and takes it and takes it — and all the audience is with him when he finally gives the guy a judo chop. What the audience wants we try to give, in a medium where you must attract at least fifteen million, and ten million is a failure.[17]

But another pointed out that violence is not the only or necessary way of attracting a large audience:

I saw *Easy Rider* and despised most of it, while recognizing that it reflects the concerns of young people. The violence at the end is ghastly in a visually disturbing way. Rednecked bigots blow the long-haired kids off their motorcycle, which turns over and over and explodes. This was last year's box office hit — along with , *Love Bug,* which is diametrically opposed in nature.[18]

While nowhere near universal, there is an ethos among the American media men which asserts 'We aren't going to get rid of violence until we get rid of advertisers.' However, as we have seen, this ethos is not fully effective since television violence is cyclical and has not increased steadily over time. This is partly explained on the basis that each organisation has a 'brake' and an 'accelerator'. The brake is the censor's office of the television company which is there to control the upward limit of the amount and type of violence whereas the 'accelerator' is the programme department which naturally wishes to maximise the audience for certain, if not all, programmes. It would be wrong to assume that the writer of a series produces his 'creation' which is then subject to the controls of brake and accelerator. The process can involve self censorship which accepts the structures of the counterposed forces without actually violating the requirements of each of these processes. One writer has said 'There are unseen fences, never discussed; after being pulled back a few times, you know instinctively how far to go'. Because a writer is only paid for completed scripts and not for rewrites and alterations, it is not in his interest to produce a too violent script which the censor or producer will ask to be rewritten.

This is not to say that there is no friction between the creative and control aspects of TV violence. Sometimes the censors appear foolish in the eyes of the producer. For example, one instance was described as follows: 'Heavies make passes at a blind girl, threaten her with a poker. She runs out into the night pursued by one of them — and Program Practices says *the girl is not to appear unduly alarmed*' (our italics). These constraints of the producer derive largely from subjective evaluations of violent scenes, and formal bases for their judgements have not been researched by the companies. For example, there are instances where taking violence 'off-camera' and implying it rather than showing it can have the effect of increasing the apparent violence of the scene. One censor described a script in which a woman was 'pulled by her hair across a room and then thrown roughly on the floor' which was eventually filmed with filing cabinets obscuring the view to meet with the censors' objections. The viewers thought that she was being raped![19]

There is no simple formula which can be applied to all violent content. Researchers have not been particularly adroit at supplying the media with information relevant to their decisions. Audience research tends not to concentrate on violence and academic research tends to deal with violence as if it were a unitary concept. Social scientists, partly due to lack of funding, have not been in a position to indicate the controls which might be implied from research findings. The codes of television content have been produced largely on the basis of the assumptions of media professionals. Whether it is worthwhile or feasible to carry out relevant research is a difficult question to answer. Obviously it is far less expensive to avoid violence altogether, but whether this is possible given the intense demands for material by the television medium is difficult to evaluate (especially bearing in mind the reliance on feature films).

WHY ARE CERTAIN PEOPLE CONCERNED?

The question of why some and not other people are concerned about violence in the mass media needs consideration if we are to understand the public debate. There are suggestions that mass media violence serves as a 'scapegoat'[20] to divert our attention from fundamental flaws in the social structure. Such arguments seem incapable of explaining why isolated individuals with no vested interest in avoiding the 'real' issues in society have complaints about the amount and sort of violence on television. It is useful, therefore, to look at some of the differences between individuals which relate to their perceptions of television and other mass media violence.

Not everyone perceives any given act of violence in exactly the same way as everyone else. This is not unexpected and points to the subjective aspect of the viewers' response to mass media violence. Equally true is the assertion that the actual number of violent encounters in a dramatic production tend not to be a good predictor of the actual perceptions of the audience of the violent content of television. For example, content analysis has shown that the rate of violent incidents per hour is four times as great for cartoon programmes[21] as for any other type of programme, whereas a study of the audience's perceptions of television violence suggests that the cartoon is not rated as a violent programme despite its 'objectively' high rate of violence.[22] While it is not possible to define exactly what the audience, in general, means by such a term, there is evidence to suggest that the audience's perceptions do not accord strongly with the objective content of programmes. For example, researchers in the BBC audience research department[23] compared objective ratings of television violence content and the viewer's personal assessment of the violence of programmes, and found little or no relationship between the objective number of violent incidents in the programmes and the proportion of viewers who rated the programme as very or quite violent. That is, one could not predict how an audience would feel about the content of a programme simply on the basis of the number of violent incidents; some qualitative rather than quantitative factors would seem to be determining audience responses. The researchers suggest on the basis of various pieces of evidence that 'By and large . . . an aggressive act was perceived as really violent only if it occurred in certain contexts and only if it was portrayed in one of a limited number of ways that aroused (usually negative) emotions, for example, if it was very graphic, if it involved real people, or if it involved fictional characters with whom the viewer could identify and empathize.' The authors go on to note that 'the well-known willingness amongst viewers to overlook violence in 'Westerns' would furnish an example of this. A shooting in the context of a Western is not termed 'violence', it seems, because the incident is perceived as part of a ritualized and stereotyped story that has very little to do with reality'. These assertions begin to explain something of the characteristics of the story or programme style which determine or set limits for the audience's perceptions of television violence. It is also important to ask the question of what are

127

the characteristics of the audience which determine how television violence is perceived.

If it were found that, say, sex or social class predicted fairly well response to television violence, we would be in a position to say something about the origins of such perceptions. Greenberg and Gordon[24] chose to concentrate largely on social class and racial differences in the perceptions of violence by adolescent boys. They assume that social class and race (black versus white) might differentiate perceptions of violence on the supposition that Negroes and lower class youths are more familiar with violence in their immediate environment and thus might be more accustomed to high levels of violence, which would result in their rating violence less extremely. While some support for this comes from the finding that the lower class and black child perceives violence as being more realistic than the more socially advantaged child, there was no evidence that the lower class child perceived less violence in a violent situation and no consistent evidence to suggest that black children perceive less violence than white children. The perceived acceptability, professed enjoyment, and perceived humour of television violence seemed to differentiate between racial and social groups rather better than did perceived violence.

Clearly experience with real life violence is not a very useful predictor of response to television violence. While one presumes with good reason that such outspoken critics as members of the Viewers and Listeners Association are by and large middle class individuals, this is but scratching the surface of the total complexity of differential perceptions.

We need systematic and far ranging investigations of the determinants of the audience's response to television violence. Ann Searle[25] has given us a start in this direction in her study of the determinants of perceptions of filmed violence in adolescents. She used teenagers' responses to the James Bond film *Goldfinger* and the film *The Comedians* based on the Graham Greene novel. Certain findings such as the tendency for boys to rate violence as less violent than did girls cannot be explained on the basis of the simple social context model propounded by Greenberg and Gordon. Several things bear on this. For example, there was no simple tendency for highly aggressive children to view the filmed violence or characters as being less violent than low aggressive children. This is quite opposed to the view that those used to violence in real life will rate filmed violence as less violent than those less often exposed. It also emerged that a rather complicated psychodynamic explanation is needed to understand the relationship between aggression and perceptions of film heroes as being aggressive. While there was no correlation between either the aggressiveness of an individual or his self-perceptions as being aggressive and his ratings of the aggressiveness of characters in a film, there was evidence of an interaction between actual aggressiveness and self-perceptions on perceptions of aggressiveness of film heroes. The individual who by an objective measure was found to be aggressive but tended not to have a self-concept of himself as being aggressive rated film characters as being more aggressive than did those who were equally aggressive but who admitted it. If it were possible to generalise, one would suggest that those who were unable to come to terms with their own aggressiveness see the most violence in film characters. Perhaps this is related to an observation from group discussions that 'Some of the individuals who expressed concern about the amount of violence shown on television seemed to be projecting their own fears or their own hostility, i.e., they were expressing aspects of their own personality charactersistics rather than appraising the situtation objectively.[26]

One should not jump too readily from these empirical findings to the conclusion that those concerned about television violence need first of all to get their own house in order, since there are many possible motivations for concern about television and other mass media violence which are as yet unexplored. The study is intriguing nevertheless. In order to understand more about the nature of the complaints against the mass media and the age old concern with the effects of media violence, it would seem important to study the sociological, psychological, and political bases for these complaints and 'protest groups'. This is not an easy task but the evidence thus far suggests that efforts in these directions should be profitable.

CONCLUSIONS AND RESERVATIONS ON
THE MEDIA VIOLENCE ISSUE

The argument that the mass media have no effect on the level of violence in society is based on several different sorts of research evidence — laboratory experiments, field experiments, and correlational field studies. The experimental method is potentially the ideal form of research to evaluate the effects of television because it offers evidence of cause (not simply correlation) but there are very definite limits on its usefulness. For example, we have seen that the laboratory experiments seem to be subject to demand characteristic explanations, to be subtly incompatible, to be accountable in terms of physiological arousal, and to be little related to the social and cultural context in which the media and violence occur. None of these factors in themselves necessarily *disprove* that vicarious violence increases the willingness of the viewer to aggress, but they do, as a whole, tend to form a coherent argument against this view. While, to some extent, field experiments deal with rather more socially relevant variables — measures of realistic interpersonal aggression, real and complete television programmes and films — a degree of artificiality remains (if to no greater extent than in many other methodologies such as surveys). The field experiments in general do not confirm the aggregate, if unreliable, conclusions from the laboratory experiments in this area. The correlational field studies when organised systematically medium by medium seem best interpreted in terms of the functions of the different media rather than in terms of the effect of violent content.

Our discussion in Chapter Four of the commonly postulated intermediary processes bringing about the effects of media violence suggests little or no evidence to confirm that imitation, identification, triggering, and so forth mediate the 'adverse effects' of the mass media. This further diminishes confidence in the already implausible hypothesis of the adverse effects of media violence. Thus we conclude that, as far as is scientifically ascertained, violence in the mass media has no effect on violence in real life.

This interpretation of the research literature does have, of course, distinct bounds. These limitations are very much to do with the nature of the evidence on which our interpretation is based but they in no way invalidate the important implications of our argument. The following are the most pressing of the reservations:

1. We have concentrated by and large on fictional presentations of violence. Some would wish to assert that it is the news and documentary presentations of violence which are the most likely sources of real life aggression in the audience rather than *Tom and Jerry* cartoons, Westerns, and so forth. A few studies have been carried out which deal with real life as opposed to fictional violence, realistic as opposed to stylised violence, but with the topic so under-researched, definite conclusions are impossible although the available data tends to indicate that these distinctions are relatively unimportant.[27] On the other hand, common sense would tell us that there are circumstances in which documentary violence in the mass media leads to real life killings. Clark and Blankenburg[28] give the example of the Kent University killings where students demonstrating against the U.S. invasion of Cambodia died as a result of the actions of peace-making agencies. Most people tend to hear of such events such as the Cambodian invasion through the mass media, not through word of mouth or by directly witnessing the event.

   In a sense then, the mass media are implicated in the Kent University deaths as an important part of the chain or communications. The cautious argument would be that circumstances were ripe for a demonstration in any case and that the mass media merely gave them a theme and an excuse, but in any case this example of a media/violence link remains beyond our frame of reference.

2. It cannot be overemphasised that the studies we have dealt with do not cover every conceivable sort of mass media violence. For

example, the laboratory studies have used a very narrow selection of films — a knife fight scene from one film, a boxing scene from another, a *Woody Woodpecker* cartoon, and so forth. The correlational and experimental field studies using naturalistic media fare still deal with a limited range of violent situations. After all, what goes on the television screen has by and large already filtered through different censoring processes — formal or implicit. The writer may not have let his ideas extend beyond what is conventional in the medium, the producer may have altered the script, the script may have been referred to third parties and amended on this basis, and so on.[29] In a sense then, our assertions are only valid for the mass media *as we know them* and may be irrelevant to future structures and different content. We can only talk about the current realities of the media and it is dangerous to go further than this. Although our limited theoretical assumptions would lead us to the view that no sorts of fictional violence are likely to make the audience more aggressive this takes us some way from the empirical data on which our theoretical assumptions are based. Caution is therefore in order.

3. The studies we have discussed take place within the context of an already existing media system. Even the earliest of the empirical investigations post-dates the mass media and mass media violence by many years and even centuries. All the investigations take place within the context of a relatively large amount of 'ambient' media violence, and the empirical studies discussed by a large number of researchers consider the relative effects of 'varying' a fairly small and (relative to the baseline media violence) insignificant amount of media violence. It is possible, therefore, that whatever effects media violence has, have already permeated society and the small variation of violence with which researchers deal is unlikely to have any effect. Hannah pouring more water on a drowning man has no effect — the poor chap is drowning anyway whether or not she does her worst.

4. Just as the range of films and violent programmes are limited, there are also considerable limitations on the scope of the aggressive and violent effects measured. Shocks on a shock generator, rude comments on a questionnaire, parental ratings of aggression, teacher ratings of violence, peer ratings of aggression, delinquent activity and so forth, although apparently far-reaching, far from describe the range of behaviours of interest.

5. A final point covers a related issue and refers to the limited way in which the causes of aggression have been examined. The research we have been concerned with examines the willingness of an individual to behave aggressively following exposure to aggressive films. Such a perspective ignores completely the social

context of aggression. Violence in society is subject to many controls — the susceptibility of victims to attack, the behaviour and presence of victims, and the activity of the police and the judiciary. To understand fully the role of the media we need to know far more about aggression in this social context.[30]

Throughout we have concentrated our attention on the empirical evidence which bears on the effects of television violence. It is not that we would wish to ignore the various speculations that have been made about the effects of mass media violence but only, as our preliminary chapters have shown, that these conceptions rarely form a coherent perspective on the topic. Inevitably, discussion of empirical data allows plenty of opportunity for subjective assessment to creep in. What seems inescapable, however, is that media research into violence fails not through lack of effort but because it has too often been fragmentary, unsystematic, and ill-conceived. Perhaps the achievement of the present account is that it unifies an apparently conflicting body of research using empirical and theoretical developments to tie together what in the past have seemed to be loose ends. Embarrassments to our account — data which do not fall readily into the proposed framework — are infrequent if not negligible.

It has to be admitted that certain sorts of evidence which have, in the past, formed the bulwark of the 'media cause violence' assertion receive rather less emphasis in our account. This is particularly true of the laboratory experiments of the Berkowitz and Bandura schools. However, these have not simply been rejected on the basis that they do not adequately resemble real life, but for the more positive reasons that the empirical validity, the inter-study generalisability, and the laboratory-field comparability of the studies are all questionable. Ultimately only time and further research will tell us whether our apparently reasonable rejection of certain sorts of evidence is appropriate. On the other hand, as our position is better supported by both experimental and correlational methodologies, it seems unlikely that particular artifacts of any sort of procedure are unduly influencing our conclusions.

The challenge to those who wish to disagree with our interpretation is not an easy one. They must produce evidence of the soundness of their methodologies, evidence which covers a wide range of media and social contexts and which integrates the plethora of apparently contradictory findings. The task would seem to be daunting.

One of the strengths of the present approach is that it fits in readily with the findings of mass communication research in general rather than standing out like a sore thumb against the now fairly substantial literature on the effects of the mass media. Of course one cannot be sure in advance that because the mass media appear to be ineffective in one area that this means they will be ineffective in others.

As suggested earlier in this chapter, research on the mass media and violence should not stop here. There are many other critical issues concerning mass media violence which go beyond the question of its effects on real life violence. Before we can have an effective understanding of the role of violence in the mass media, it is important to extend our knowledge of its functions, the reasons for its emphasis, and the need for control.

Perhaps research should not progress quite so blindly as it has done in the past. It would be ideal if research was designed to answer the practical problems of the programme producer and the executive interested in the formation of policy with respect to television violence, as well as those more politically concerned with the issue. Simple questions, such as whether mass media violence causes violence in real life, often have little to say about what should be done about it if this were indeed found to be the case. What sorts of media violence might cause real life violence is a better question. Also, there are so many issues involved in any policy decision that the researcher should be more aware of the complexities when he is formulating his research hypotheses and methodologies. Increased cooperation between researcher and practitioner would aid in this synthesis.

Research is not so highly valued by many sections of society as it might be, partly because of the frequent failure of researchers to deliver the goods, but also because social policy decisions are often so poorly formulated as to be incapable of effectively utilising even the most excellent research. Even this is an oversimplification in that research is as subject to political influences of various sorts as any other aspect of society. For example, research sometimes serves the function of giving the impression that 'something is being done about' a social problem without any decisions actually having to be made; in this way, doing research can often be a substitute for action.

It is of great concern to us that some of the criticisms and comments we have made about particular pieces of research throughout the book will cause some readers to conclude that research is of necessity frivolous, ill-thought out, and a waste of valuable resources. This is not our intention at all. While we would not deny that some of the research which has been deemed relevant to the issue of the effects of the mass media in the past falls far short of the ideal, it is on these very building blocks that our account, for what it is worth, rests. One would not wish to defend every last piece of research on the grounds that it contributed something to the whole, but a lot of what we have written emphasises that no single piece of research can be regarded as a definitive answer to any social problem. To some extent it is incumbent on social science to be meticulous in replicating, testing and challenging since this is, or should be, the very core of the social scientific approach. If we have shown some of the limitations imposed by methodology on the social scientist we have begun to show why social science takes a long time to answer apparently simple questions and why one seems to get so little in return for a comparatively large capital outlay.

However, the ball is not in the researcher's court alone. The researcher cannot be expected to come up with insights about the mass media if obstacles are not removed. A good example of this is the need for broadcasters actively to encourage researchers to investigate the structures and pressures within the broadcasting organisation which help to control media output. Earlier in this chapter we showed that it is no accident that the mass media rely on violence as a central aspect of their programming. We may question whether such preoccupations are inevitable and whether the broadcasting institutions are sufficiently sensitive to the needs and wishes of the viewing public. To begin to answer the question of media violence we must look considerably further than an individual's act of aggression. We must ask about the social context of aggression. We must have a clear documentation of the relationship between the media products and the media organisations which produce and transmit them. Ultimately we must ask about the very nature and structure of media organisations, the needs which they serve and the kinds of audience which they attract or repel. This is a far cry from simply demanding to know the effects of violence in the mass media.

CHAPTER NOTES AND REFERENCES

NOTES TO CHAPTER 1.

1. S. Butler, *Erewhon,* Chapter 20.
2. F. Teer and J.D. Spence. (1973). *Political Opinion Polls,* Methuen, London.
   C.W. Roll and A.H. Cantril (1972). *Polls,* Basic Books, New York.
3. G. Cumberbatch. *The Mass Media and Northern Ireland,* in preparation.
4. Opinion Research Centre. (1973). *The Sunday Times,* 25.2.1973.
5. H. Himmelweit, A.N. Openheim and P. Vince. (1958). *Television and the Child,* Oxford University Press, London.
   W. Schramm, J. Lyle and E.B. Parker. (1961). *Television in the Lives of Our Children,* Stanford University Press, Stanford, Calif.
6. Gallup Polls Ltd. (1968). Social Surveys. *Polls,* 111(3).
7. R.S. Randall. (1968). *Censorship of the movies,* University of Wisconsin Press, Madison, Wisconsin.
8. J.D. Halloran, R.L. Brown and D. Chaney. (1970). *Television and Delinquency,* Leicester University Press, Leicester.
9. M. Gurevitch. (1972). 'The Structure and Content of Television Broadcasting in Four Countries', in *Television and Social Behavior, Volume 1.* Eds. G.A. Comstock and E.A. Rubinstein, U.S. Government Printing Office, Washington, D.C. pp. 374-385. See also Chapter 2 for a review of the content analysis research.
10. Bureau of Social Science Research. (1967). *See* 12. below for a review.
11. K. Thomas. (Ed.). (1971). *Attitudes and Behaviour,* Penguin, Harmondsworth.
12. J. McIntyre. (1967). Public Attitudes Towards Crime and Law Enforcement. *The Annals, 374* (November) pp. 34-46.
13. *The Times,* 28.7.1970. Press report.
14. R. Roshier. (1969). *Crime and the Press,* unpublished PhD Thesis, University of Newcastle, Newcastle.
15. J.B. Haskins. (1969). The Effects of Violence in the Printed Media, in *Mass Media and Violence,* Eds. R.K. Baker and S. Ball. U.S. Government Printing Office, Washington, D.C.
16. *See* for example, *Report of the Committee on Broadcasting* (1960), HMSO, London.

Independent Broadcasting Authority Annual Report and Accounts 1972-73, Independent Broadcasting Authority, London.
17. *The Observer* 15.3.1970.
18. *The Observer* 15.3.1970.
19. *London Day,* March 1969.
20. J. Galtung and M.H. Ruge (1965). The Structure of Foreign News. *Journal of International Peace Research, 1,* 64-90.
21. G. Cumberbatch and D. Howitt (1974). 'Social Communication and War', in *La Communication Sociale et la Guerre,* Editions Bruylant, Bruxelles, pp. 127-142.
22. L.T. Wilkins. (1964). *Social Deviance,* Tavistock, London.
23. N.H. Avison. (1972). 'Criminal Statistics as Social Indicators', in *Social Indicators and Social Policy,* Ed. A. Shonfield, Heinneman, London.

NOTES TO CHAPTER 2.

1. Data from *Future of Broadcasting* study, ongoing, at Centre for Mass Communication Research, University of Leicester.
2. *See* for example, R.B. Bechtel, C. Achelpohl, and R. Akers. (1971). 'Correlates between Observed Behavior and Questionnaire Responses on Television Viewing', in *Television and Social Behavior, Volume 4, Television in Day-to-Day Life: Patterns of Use* Eds. E.A. Rubinstein, G.A. Comstock and J.P. Murray, U.S. Government Printing Office, Washington, D.C. pp.274-344.
3. W. Schramm, J. Lyle, and E. Parker. (1961). *Television in the Lives of Our Children,* Stanford University Press.
4. H. Israel and J.P. Robinson. (1971). 'Demographic Characteristics of Viewers of Television Violence and News Programs', in *Television and Social Behavior, Volume 4, Television in Day-to-Day Life: Patterns of Use.* Eds. E.A. Rubinstein, G.A. Comstock and J.P. Murray, U.S. Government Printing Office, Washington, D.C. pp.87-128.
5. F. Wertham. (1954). *Seduction of the Innocent,* Rinehart, New York. F. Wertham. (1962). 'The Scientific Study of Mass Media Effects', *American Journal of Psychiatry,* 119, 306-311.
6. H.J. Foreman. (1935). *Our Movie Made Children,* Macmillan, New York, p.38.
7. D.G. Clark and W.B. Blankenburg. (1971). 'Trends in Violent Content in Selected Mass Media', in *Television and Social Behavior, Volume 1, Content and Control,* Eds. G.A. Comstock and E.A. Rubinstein. U.S. Government Printing Office, Washington, D.C. pp. 188-243.
8. G. Gerbner. (1971). 'Violence in Television Drama: Trends and Symbolic Functions' in *Television and Social Behavior. Volume 1. Content and Control.* Eds. G.A. Comstock and E.A. Rubinstein,

U.S. Government Printing Office, Washington D.C., pp. 28-187

R.K. Baker and S.J. Ball (1969). 'The Television World of Violence', in *Violence and the Media* Eds. R.K. Baker and S.J. Ball, U.S. Government Printing Office, Washington D.C., pp. 311-38.

9. Unpublished data from *Future of Broadcasting Study*, Centre for Mass Communication Research, University of Leicester, Leicester.
10. J.D. Halloran and P. Croll. (1971). 'Television Programs in Great Britain: Content and Control', in *Television and Social Behavior, Volume 1.* Eds. G.A. Comstock and E.A. Rubinstein, U.S. Government Printing Office, Washington D.C. pp.415-92.
11. See Note 8.
12. W. Schramm, J. Lyle, and E. Parker. (1961). *Television in the Lives of Our Children,* Stanford University Press, pp.139-40.
13. See Note 10.
14. D. Howitt and G. Cumberbatch. (1974). 'Audience Perceptions of Violent Television Content', *Communications Research,* in Press.
15. R.K. Baker and S.J. Ball. (1969). 'The Television World of Violence', in *Violence and the Media* Eds. R.K. Baker and S.J. Ball, U.S. Government Printing Office, Washington, D.C. p.338.
16. J. Klapper. (1960). *The Effects of Mass Communication* Free Press, Glencoe, p.8.
17. See, for example, J. Klapper. (1960). *The Effects of Mass Communication,* Free Press, Glencoe. However, there are distinct limits to the generality of this argument, such as those reported in D. Howitt (1975), 'The Effects of Television on Children', in *Children and Television,* Ed. R. Brown, Collier MacMillan, London.
18. R.K. Baker and S.J. Ball. (1969). 'The Actual World of Violence', in *Violence and the Media,* Eds. R.K.Baker and S.J. Ball, U.S. Government Printing Office, Washington, D.C., pp.341-62.
19. This is so despite several recent books and summaries, e.g. A. Bandura (1973). *Aggression,* Prentice Hall, New York.
20. J.D. Halloran. (1970). *Effects of Television,* Panther, London.
21. See Note 18.
22. Some of these are listed in Note 19 of Chapter 3.

NOTES TO CHAPTER 3

1. Reviews of the notion of catharsis are provided by:
   R. Goranson. (1969). 'The Catharsis Effect: Two Opposing Views'. pp.453-59.
   S. Feshbach. (1969). 'The Catharsis Effect: Research and Another View'. pp.461-72.
   Both in *Mass Media and Violence,* Eds. R. Baker and S. Ball, U.S. Government Printing Office, Washington D.C.
2. This sort of argument has been suggested by Albert Bandura.
3. Studies of the effects of punishment on imitation include:

137

A. Bandura, D. Ross and S. Ross. (1963). Vicarious Reinforcement and Imitative Learning, *Journal of Abnormal and Social Psychology,* **67**, 527-34.

D. Hicks. (1968), 'Short- and Long-Term Retention of Affectively Varied Modeled Behavior', *Psychonomic Science,* **11**, 369-70.

4. This has been called, variously, stimulation, disinhibition, cueing and enhancement.

5. The reason for this caution stems from the fact that it is impossible to prove, ultimately, that media violence has no effects since there are many circumstances which may not have been investigated.

6. The idea of aggression anxiety as an explanation of 'catharsis' effects appears early, e.g. L. Berkowitz. (1960). 'Some Factors Affecting the Reduction of Overt Hostility' *Journal of Abnormal and Social Psychology,* **60**, 41-21.

7. L. Berkowitz and E. Rawlings. (1963). 'Effects of Film Violence on Subsequent Aggressive Tendencies', *Journal of Abnormal and Social Psychology*, **66**, 405-12.

   L. Berkowitz, R. Corwin and M. Hieronimus. (1963). 'Film Violence and Subsequent Aggressive Tendencies', *Public Opinion Quarterly*, **27**, 217-229.

8. *See* Note 7.

9. S. Feshbach. (1961). 'The Stimulating Versus Cathartic Effects of a Vicarious Aggressive Activity', *Journal of Abnormal and Social Psychology*, **63**, 381-85.

10. *See* Note 7.

11. These possibilities have not been pursued empirically to date.

12. *See* Note 9.

13. *See* Note 7.

14. That is, the evidence from Berkowitz's studies was not really compatible with that from the Feshbach study since the essential elements of Feshbach's study failed to emerge in the high aggression anxiety condition.

15. R. Walters and E. Thomas. (1963). 'Enhancement of Punitiveness by Visual and Audio-Visual Displays', *Canadian Journal of Psychology,* **17**, 244-55.

    R. Walters, E. Thomas and C. Acker. (1962). 'Enhancement of Punitive Behavior by Audio-Visual Displays', *Science,* **136**, 873-73.

16. A. Buss. (1961). *The Psychology of Aggression,* Wiley, New York.

17. Not only that, but it is clearly possible that the control film was depressing aggression levels rather than the violent film increasing them, since no control was included in which no film at all was shown. We return to this at the end of the chapter. We follow the original authors in using such terms as stimulation even though this may be misleading. *See* W. Weiss. (1969). 'Effects of the Mass

Media of Communication', in *The Handbook of Social Psychology*, Eds. G. Lindzey and E. Aronson, Addison-Wesley, Reading, Mass. p.141.

18. For details see the second part of Feshbach's hypothesis quoted earlier in the chapter.

19. The following lists some of the experiments in this tradition and notes the measures used:

Projective Measures

These use the Thematic Apperception Test and similar measures.

R.S. Albert. (1957). 'The Role of Mass Media and the Effect of Aggressive Film Content upon Children's Aggressive Responses and Identification Choices', *Genetic Psychology Monographs,* **55,** 221-85.

L. Ancona. (1963). 'The Film as an Element in the Dynamics of Aggressiveness', *Revue Internationale de Filmologie,* **13,** 29-33.

L. Ancona and M. Fontanesi. (1967). 'Analisi delle Relazioni Dinamiche tra Effetto, Catartico ed Effetto Frustrante de uno Stimolo Cinematografico Emotive', *Contributi Dell'Instituto di Psicologia,* **28,** 30-48.

F. Emery. (1959). 'Psychological Effects of the Western Film: A Study in Television Viewing: II, The Experimental Study', *Human Relations,* **12,** 215-32.

F. Emery and D. Martin. (1957). *Psychological Effects of the "Western" Film,* Department of Audio-Visual Aids, University of Melbourne.

N. Goldstein. (1956). *The Effect of Animated Cartoons on Hostility in Children ,* Unpublished doctoral dissertation, New York University.

N. Rosenthal. (1962). 'Crime and Violence in Television Programmes: Their Impact on Children and Adolescents', *Audio Visual Aids Review,* **3 (2)** 5-9.

N. Rosenthal. (1963). 'Crime et Violence dans les Programmes de Television', *Revue Internationale de Filmologie,* **13,**85-91.

R. Thomson. (1959). *Television Crime Drama: Its Impact on Children and Adolescents,* F.W. Cheshire, Melbourne.

Electric Shocks or Adverse Reports

L. Berkowitz. (1964). 'The Effects of Observing Violence', *Scientific American,* **210** 35-41.

L. Berkowitz. (1965). 'The Concept of Aggressive Drive: Some Additional Considerations', in *Advances in Experimental Social Psychology,* Volume 2, Ed. L. Berkowitz, Academic Press, New York, pp.301-29.

L. Berkowitz. (1965), 'Some Aspects of Observed Aggression', *Journal of Personality and Social Psychology,* **2,** 359-69.

L. Berkowitz. (1967), 'Experiments on Automatism and Intent in

Human Aggression', in *Aggression and Defence (Brain Function, Volume 5)*, Eds. C.D. Clemente and D.B. Lindsley, University of California Press, Berkeley and Los Angeles, pp.242-66.

L. Berkowitz. (1970). 'The Contagion of Violence: An S-R Mediational Analysis of Some Effects of Observed Aggression', in *Nebraska Symposium on Motivation*, Eds. W.J. Arnold and M.M. Page, University of Nebraska Press, Lincoln, pp.95-135.

L. Berkowitz and J.T. Alioto. (1973). 'The Meaning of an Observed Event as a Determinant of Its Aggressive Consequences', *Journal of Personality and Social Psychology,* **28 (2)** 206-17.

L. Berkowitz, R. Corwin and M. Hieronimus. (1963). 'Film Violence and Subsequent Aggressive Tendencies', *Public Opinion Quarterly*, **27**, 217-29.

L. Berkowitz and R.G. Geen. (1966). 'Film Violence and the Cue Properties of Available Targets', *Journal of Personality and Social Psychology*, **3**, 525-30.

L. Berkowitz and R.G. Geen. (1967), 'Stimulus Qualities of the Target of Aggression: A Further Study', *Journal of Personality and Social Psychology*, **5**, 364-68.

L. Berkowitz and D. Knurek. (1969), 'Label-Mediated Hostility Generalization', *Journal of Personality and Social Psychology*, **13**, 200-6.

L. Berkowitz, R.D. Parke, J. Leyens, and S.G. West. (1973). *Reactions of Juvenile Delinquents to 'Justified' and 'Less Justified' Movie Violence.* Unpublished Manuscript, Department of Psychology, University of Wisconsin.

L. Berkowitz and E. Rawlings. (1963). 'Effects of Film Violence on Subsequent Aggressive Tendencies', *Journal of Abnormal and Social Psychology*, **66**, 405-12.

S. Feshbach. (1961). 'The Stimulating Versus Cathartic Effects of a Vicarious Aggressive Activity', *Journal of Abnormal and Social Psychology*, **63**, 381-85.

S. Feshbach. (1971). Reality and Fantasy in Filmed Violence', in *Television and Social Behaviour, Volume 2: Television and Social Learning*, Eds. J.P. Murray, E.A. Rubinstein and G.A. Comstock, U.S. Government Printing Office, Washington, D.C.

R.G. Geen and L. Berkowitz. (1966). 'Name Mediated Aggressive Cue Properties', *Journal of Personality*, **34**, 456-65.

R.G. Geen and L. Berkowitz. (1967). 'Some Conditions Facilitating the Occurrence of Aggression After the Observation of Violence', *Journal of Personality*, **35**, 666-76.

R.E. Goranson. (1970). *Observed Violence and Aggressive Behaviour: The Effects of Negative Outcomes to the Observed Violence*, Unpublished Doctoral Dissertation. Ann Arbor, Michigan, University Microfilms, 70-8286.

D.P. Hartmann. (1969). *The Influence of Symbolically Modeled Instrumental Aggressive and Pain Cues on the Disinhibition of Aggressive Behaviour*. Unpublished Doctoral Dissertation, University of California, Stanford, Ann Arbor, Michigan. University Microfilms, 65-12789.

D. Hartmann. (1969). 'Influence of Symbolically Modeled Instrumental Aggression and Pain Cues on Aggressive Behaviour', *Journal of Personality and Social Psychology*, **11**, 280-88.

J.L. Hoyt. (1967). *Vengence and Self-Defence as Justification for Filmed Aggression*, unpublished Masters Thesis, University of Wisconsin.

J.L. Hoyt. (1970). 'Effect of Media Violence "Justification" on Aggression', *Journal of Broadcasting*, **14**, 455-64.

R.C. Johnson. (1971). *Seldom Tested Variables in the Effects of Televised Violence on Aggressive Behavior*. Unpublished Doctoral Dissertation, Ohio University. Ann Arbor, Michigan, University Microfilms, 72-9587.

R. Liebert and R. Baron. (1971). 'Short-Term Effects of Televised Aggression on Children's Aggressive Behavior', in *Television and Social Behavior, Volume 2, Television and Social Learning*, Eds. J.P. Murray, E.A. Rubinstein and G.A. Comstock, U.S. Government Printing Office, Washington, D.C.

T.P. Meyer. (1971). 'Some Effects of Real Newsfilm on the Behavior of Viewers', *Journal of Broadcasting*, **15**, 275-85.

T.P. Meyer. (1972). 'Effects of Viewing Justified and Unjustified Real Film Violence on Aggressive Behavior', *Journal of Personality and Social Psychology*, **23**, 21-29.

L. Meyerson. (1966). *The Effects of Filmed Aggression on the Aggressive Responses of High and Low Aggressive Subjects*, Unpublished Doctoral Dissertation, University of Iowa.

R.W. Silverman. (1972). *Short Term Effects of Television on Aggressive and Psychophysiological Behavior of Adults and Children*, Unpublished Doctoral Dissertation, State University of New York at Buffalo. Ann Arbor, Michigan, University Microfilms, 73-5174.

R.E. Stoessel. (1972). *The Effects of Televised Aggressive Cartoons on Children's Behavior*. Unpublished Doctoral Dissertation, St. John's University. Ann Arbor, Michigan, University Microfilms, 72-21736.

R. Walters and E. Thomas. (1963). 'Enhancement of Punitiveness by Visual and Audio-Visual Displays', *Canadian Journal of Psychology*, **17**, 244-55.

R. Walters, E. Thomas and C. Acker. (1962). 'Enhancement of Punitive Behavior by Audio-Visual Displays', *Science*, **136** 872-73.

Experiments using other types of measure of Aggression:

G. Ellis and F. Sekyra. (1972). 'The Effect of Aggressive Cartoons on the Behavior of First Grade Children', *Journal of Psychology*, **81**, 37-43, Observers' ratings of aggression.

D. Heyman. (1969), *The Effect of Film Mediated Aggression on Subsequent Aggressive Behavior*, Unpublished Doctoral dissertation, University of Connecticut, Effects of filmed aggression on verbal aggression zero.

O.I. Lövaas. (1961). 'Effect of Exposure to Symbolic Aggression on Aggressive Behavior', *Child Development*, **32**, 37-44. In one of three experiments children used aggressive model more if watched aggressive film.

D.L. Larder. (1962). 'Effect of Aggressive Story Content on Nonverbal Play Behaviour', *Psychological Reports*, **11**, 14. Effect of reading an aggressive story on the child's willingness to use an 'aggressive' model.

P.H. Mussen and E. Rutherford. (1961). 'Effects of Aggressive Cartoons on Children's Aggressive Play', *Journal of Abnormal and Social Psychology*, **62**, 461-64. After watching aggressive cartoon children more willing to say that they would like to 'pop' a balloon.

G. Noble. (1970). 'Film Mediated Creative and Aggressive Play', *British Journal of Social and Clinical Psychology*, **9**, 1-7.

G. Noble. (1973). 'Effects of Different Forms of Filmed Aggression on Children's Constructive and Destructive Play', *Journal of Personality and Social Psychology*, **26**, (1), 54-59.

Both of these articles deal with the effects of filmed aggression on the constructiveness and destructiveness of play as rated by observers.

C.E. Wotring. (1971). *The Effects of Exposure to Television Violence on Adolescents' Verbal Aggression*. Michigan State University. Ann Arbor, Michigan, University Microfilms, 72-16542. Measured five types of verbal aggression and one type of physical — no effects due to films.

20. There are signs in the recent reports on violence published by the Independent Broadcasting Authority that they are beginning to accept that sanitised violence may not be different from any other form of violence in its effects.

21. D. Hartmann. (1969). *The Influence of Symbolically Modeled Instrumental Aggressive and Pain Cues on the Disinhibition of Aggressive Behavior.* Unpublished doctoral dissertation, University of California, Stanford. Ann Arbor, Michigan, University Microfilms 65-12789.

D. Hartmann. (1969). 'Influence of Symbolically Modeled Instrumental Aggression and Pain Cues on Aggressive Behaviour', *Journal of Personality and Social Psychology*, **11** 280-88.

22. R. Goranson. (1970). *Observed Violence and Aggressive Behavior: The Effects of Negative Outcomes to the Observed Violence*, Unpublished doctoral dissertation. Ann Arbor, Michigan, University Microfilms, 70-8286.

23. L. Meyerson. (1966). *The Effects of Filmed Aggression on the Aggressive Responses of High and Low Aggressive Subjects*. Unpublished doctoral dissertation, University of Iowa.

24. S. Feshbach and R. Singer. (1971). *Television and Aggression*, Jossey-Bass, San Franciso. Also, S. Feshbach. (1969). 'The Catharsis Effect: Research and Another View', in *Mass Media and Violence,* Eds. R. Baker and S. Ball, U.S. Government Printing Office, Washington, D.C., pp.461-72.

25. Literature discussing the Feshbach and Singer study includes:
    R. Liebert, M. Sobol and E. Davidson. (1971). 'Television and Aggression: Discussion', pp.351-59.
    S. Feshbach and R. Singer. (1971). 'Television and Aggression: A Reply to Leibert, Sobol and Davidson', pp.359-66.
    R. Liebert, E. Davidson and M. Sobol. (1971). 'Catharsis of Aggression Among Institutionalized Boys: Further Comments', pp.366-73.
    S. Feshbach and R. Singer (1971). 'Television and Aggression: Some Reactions to the Liebert,Sobol and Davidson Review and Responses', pp.373-75.
    All the above are in *Television and Social Behavior, Volume V: Television's Effects: Further Explorations,* Eds. G.A. Comstock, E.A. Rubinstein and J.P. Murrary, U.S. Government Printing Office, Washington, D.C.

26. See discussion of Page and Scheidt study towards the end of this chapter.

27. W. Wells. (1973). *Television and Aggression: Replication of an Experimental Field Study*. Unpublished manuscript, Graduate School of Business, University of Chicago.

28. S. Ball-Rokeach. (1971). 'Review of Television and Aggression by S. Feshbach and R.D. Singer', *Public Opinion Quarterly,* **35,** 501-4.

29 A. Stein and L. Friedrich. (1971). 'Television Content and Young Children's Behaviour', in *Television and Social Behavior, Volume II,* Eds. J.P. Murray, E.A. Rubinstein and G.A. Comstock, U.S. Government Printing Office, Washington, D.C.
    L. Friedrich and A. Stein. (1973). 'Aggressive and Prosocial Television Programs and the Natural Behavior of Preschool Children', *Monographs of the Society for Research in Child Development,* 151, 38, No.4.

30. Personal Communication from A. Stein.

31. F. Steuer, J. Applefield and S.R. Smith. (1971). 'Televised Aggression and the Interpersonal Aggression of Pre-school

Children', *Journal of Experimental Child Psychology*, **11**, 422-47.

32. W. Hapkiewicz and A. Roden. (1971). 'The Effect of Aggressive Cartoons on Children's Interpersonal Play', *Child Development*, **42**, 1583-85.

33. R.D. Parke, L. Berkowitz, J.P. Leyens, S. West, and R.J. Sebastian. (1974). *Film Violence and Aggression: A Field Experimental Analysis,* unpublished manuscript, University of Wisconsin.

34. J.P. Leyens, L. Camino. R.D. Parke and L. Berkowitz. (1974). *The Effects of Movie Violence on Aggression in a Field Setting as a Function of Group Dominance and Cohesion*, unpublished manuscript, University of Louvain.
    J.P. Leyens and L. Camino. (1974). 'The Effects of Social Structures and Repeated Exposure to Film Violence on Aggression', in *Determinants and Origins of Aggressive Behaviour*, Eds. W.W. Hartup and J. Dewit, Mouton, The Hague.

35. A. Siegel. (1956). Film-Mediated Fantasy Aggression and Strength of Aggressive Drive, *Child Development*, **27**, 365-78.

36. J. Klapper. (1960). *The Effects of Television*. The Free Press, Glencoe.
    Also C. Hovland. (1959). 'Reconciling Conflicting Results Derived from Experimental and Survey Studies of Attitude Change', *American Psychologist*, **14**, 18-27.

37. Such books as *The Experimenter's Dilemma*. (1971). Ed. J. Jung. Harper and Row, New York, present introductions to this issue.

38. M. Orne. (1962). 'On the Social Psychology of the Psychological Experiment', *American Psychologist*, **17**, 776-83.
    M. Orne. (1969). 'Demand Characteristics and the Concept of Quasi-Controls', in *Artifact in Behavioral Research*, Eds. R. Rosenthal and R. Rosnow, Academic Press, New York, pp.143-79.

39 M. Orne and K. Scheibe. (1964). 'The Contribution of Nondeprivation Factors in the Production of Sensory Deprivation Effects: The Psychology of the "Panic Button"', *Journal of Abnormal and Social Psychology*, **68**, 3-12.

40. L. Levey. (1967). 'Awareness, Learning, and the Beneficient Subject as Expert Witness', *Journal of Personality and Social Psychology*, **6**, 365-70.

41. M. Page. (1970). 'Demand Awareness, Subject Sophistication, and the Effectiveness of Verbal "Reinforcement"', *Journal of Personality*, **38**, 287-301.

42. S. Golding and E. Lichtenstein. (1970). 'Confession of Awareness and Prior Knowledge of Deception as a Function of Interview Set and Approval Motivation', *Journal of Personality and Social Psychology*, **14**, 213-23.

43. There has, however, been a tendency for those accepting the hypothesis that media violence enhances aggression to suggest that

those advocating demand characteristic explanations should prove their claim, rather than regarding it as incumbent on themselves to prove theirs.

44. O. Larsen. (1968). *Violence and the Mass Media,* Harper and Row, New York. p.291.

45 M. Page and R. Scheidt. (1971). 'The Elusive Weapons Effect: Demand Awareness, Evaluation Apprehension, and Slightly Sophisticated Subjects', *Journal of Personality and Social Psychology*, **20**, 304-18.

46. L. Berkowitz and A. LePage. (1967). 'Weapons as Aggression Eliciting Stimuli', *Journal of Personality and Social Psychology*, **7**, 202-7.
   See also L. Berkowitz. (1971). 'The "Weapons Effect", Demand Charactersitics, and the Myth of the Compliant Subject', *Journal of Personality and Social Psychology*, **20**, (3), 332-8.

47. D. Howitt and G. Cumberbath. (1971). *Experiment Transparency in a Study of the Effects of Filmed Aggression* unpublished manuscript, Centre for Mass Communication Research, University of Leicester.
   J. Schuck and K. Pisor. (1974). 'Evaluating an Aggression Experiment by the Use of Simulating Subjects', *Journal of Personality and Social Psychology*, **29** (2), 181-8, reports an experiment in which subjects were instructed to behave as if the full experimental manipulation had been given. The basic design was similar to those of Berkowitz. The authors write:
   > These results offer little support for Berkowitz's basic aggression design. When shock was the dependent variable, simulating subjects did not differ significantly from real subjects. (p.185).

48. L. Berkowitz and J. Alioto. (1973). 'The Meaning of an Observed Event as a Determinant of its Aggressive Consequences', *Journal of Personality and Social Psychology*, **28**, 206-17.

49. R. Goranson. (1970). *Observed Violence and Aggressive Behavior: The Effects of Negative Outcomes to the Observed Violence*, unpublished doctoral dissertation. Ann Arbor, Michigan, University Microfilms 70-8286.

50. P. Tannenbaum. (1971). 'Studies in Film- and Television-Mediated Arousal and Aggression: A Progress Report', in *Television and Social Behavior, Volume V, Television's Effects: Further Explorations,* Eds. G.A. Comstock, E.A. Rubinstein, and J.P. Murray, U.S. Government Printing Office, Washington, D.C.

51. P. Tannenbaum. (1970). 'Emotional Arousal as a Mediator of Communication Effects', *Technical Reports of the Commission on Obscenity and Pornography* Volume 8, U.S.Government Printing

Office, Washington, D.C.

P. Tannenbaum. (1971). 'Studies of Film- and Television-Mediated Arousal and Aggression: A Progress Report', in *Television and Social Behavior, Volume V, Television's Effects: Further Explorations,* Eds. G.A. Comstock, E.A. Rubinstein and J.P. Murray, U.S. Government Printing Office, Washington, D.C. pp. 309-50.

52. For example, the early work of Bandura (discussed in next chapter) demonstrated the importance of controlling for activity level in gauging the effects of aggressive films.

53. R. Walters and M. Brown. (1964). 'A Test of the High-Magnitude Theory of Aggression', *Journal of Experimental Child Psychology*, **1**, 376-87.

54. R.G. Geen and E. O'Neal. (1969). 'Activation of Cue-Elicited Aggression by General Arousal', *Journal of Personality and Social Psychology,* **11 (3)**, 289-92.

55. P. Tannenbaum. (1971). 'Studies of Film- and Television-Mediated Arousal and Aggression: A Progress Report', in *Television and Social Behavior , Volume V, Television's Effects: Further Explorations*, Eds. G.A. Comstock, E.A. Rubinstein, and J.P. Murray, U.S. Government Printing Office, Washington, D.C. p.339.

56. D. Zillman and R. Johnson. (1973). 'Motivated Aggressiveness Perpetuated by Exposure to Aggressive Films and Reduced by Non-Aggressive Films', *Journal of Research in Personality*, **7**, 261-76.

NOTES TO CHAPTER 4

1. *See,* for example, D. Graham. (1972). *Moral Learning and Moral Development*, Batsford, London, for a review of Freud's concepts of identification.

2. It should also be noted that identification with the aggressor would exclude identification with people on other bases — e.g. pop stars.

3. A. Bandura. (1969). *Principles of Behavior Modification*, Holt, Rinehart, and Winston, New York.

4. D. Howitt and G. Cumberbatch. (1972). 'Affective feeling for a Film Character and Evaluation of an Anti-Social Act', *British Journal of Social and Clinical Psychology*, **11**, 102-8.
   D. Howitt and G. Cumberbatch. (1973). 'The Parameters of Attraction to Mass Media Figures', *Journal of Moral Education*, 2, June, 269-81.

5. We are referring, of course, to the many models of social behaviour based on consistency which appear in most Psychology texts.

6. Evidence that this is not the case for aggression is reported later in this chapter.

7. C. Houland. (1954). 'Effects of the Mass Media of Communication', in *The Handbook of Social Psychology*, Ed. G. Lindzey, Addison-Wesley, Reading, Mass. pp.1062-103.

W. Weiss. (1969). 'Effects of the Mass media on Communication', in *Handbook of Social Psychology,* Eds. G. Lindzey and E. Aronson, Addison-Wesley, Reading, Mass. pp.88-195.

8. P. Croll. (1974). Unpublished manuscript, Centre for Mass Communication Research, University of Leicester.

9. H. Blumer. (1933). *Movies and Conduct*, Macmillan, New York.
   H. Blumer and P.M. Hauser. (1933). *Movies, Delinquency and Crime,* Macmillan, New York.

10. British Broadcasting Corporation. (1962). 'Violence in Television Programmes', *Television Quarterly,* 1, 61-63.

11. W. Schramm, J. Lyle and C. Parker. (1961). *Television in the Lives of Our Children*, Stanford University Press, p.42.

12. E. Maccoby and W. Wilson. (1957). 'Identification and Observational Learning from Films', *Journal of Abnormal and Social Psychology*, 55, 76-87.

13. A. Glucksmann. (1971). *Violence on the Screen*, British Film Institute, London.

14. Any shop will demonstrate ample proof of this.

15. This is unreported data from the study reported as D. Howitt and G. Cumberbatch. (1973). 'The Parameters of Attraction to Mass Media Figures', *Journal of Moral Education,* 2 (3), 269-81.

16. D. Howitt and G. Cumberbatch. (1972). 'Affective Feeling for a Film Character and Evaluation of an Anti-Social Act', *British Journal of Social and Clinical Psychology, 11*, 102-8.

17. G. Cumberbatch and D. Howitt. (1974). 'Identification with Aggressive Television Characters and Children's Moral Judgements', in *Determinants and Origins of Aggressive Behavior,* Eds. W.W. Hartup and J. Dewit, Mouton, The Hague.

18. G. Cumberbatch and D. Howitt. (1971). *The Effects of Film Hero Identification on the Moral Values of Adolescents*. Unpublished manuscript, Centre for Mass Communication Research, University of Leicester.

19. G. Noble. (1971). 'Some Comments on the Nature of Delinquents' Identification with Television Heroes, Fathers, and Best Friends', *British Journal of Social and Clinical Psychology,* 10, 172-80.

20 J.D. Halloran, R. Brown and D. Chaney. (1970). *Television and Delinquency.* Leicester University Press, Leicester.

21 J.M. McLeod, C.K. Atkin and S.H. Chaffee. (1971). Adolescents, parents, and Television Use: Adolescent Self-Report Measures from Maryland and Wisconsin Samples, in *Television and Social Behavior, Volume III, Television and Adolescent Aggressiveness.* Eds. G.A. Comstock and E.A. Rubinstein, U.S. Government Printing Office, Washington, D.C., pp.173-238.

22. S. Milgram and L.R. Shotland. (1973). *Television and Anti-Social Behavior: Field Experiments*, Academic Press, New York.

23. C.W. Turner and L. Berkowitz. (1972). 'Identification with Film Aggression (Covert Role Taking) and Reactions to Film Violence', *Journal of Personality and Social Psychology*, **21** (2) 256-64. However, J.P. Leyens and S. Picus. (1973). 'Identification with the Winner of a Fight and Name Mediation: Their Differential Effects upon Subsequent Aggressive Behavior', *British Journal of Social and Clinical Psychology*, **12**, 374-77, carried out a very similar study and found no effects due to the instructions to identify. On the other hand, *post hoc* measures of identification yielded differences but these are very much in line with the sort of relationships found in other studies — before controls are applied. Therefore the findings of this study do not deviate from the assertion that identification is not an important mediating factor in the effects of media violence.

24. D. Howitt and G. Cumberbatch. (1971). *The Ethnology of Imitation,* unpublished manuscript, Centre for Mass Communication Research, University of Leicester.

25. E. Karp. (1954). *Crime Comic Book Role Preferences,* Unpublished doctoral dissertation, New York University.

26. E. Aronson and B.W. Golden. (1962). 'The Effect of Relevant and Irrelevant Aspects of Communicator Credibility on Opinion Change', *Journal of Personality* **30** (2) 135-46.

27. A. Bandura and A. Huston. (1961). 'Identification as a Process of Incidental Learning', *Journal of Abnormal and Social Psychology*, **63**, 311-18. But see R.A. Baron and C.R. Kepner. (1970). 'Model's Behaviour and Attraction Toward the Model as Determinants of Adult Aggressive Behavior', *Journal of Personality and Social Psychology*, **14**, 335-44.

28. D. Howitt and G. Cumberbatch. (1973). The' Parameters of Attraction to Mass Media Figures', *Journal of Moral Education*, **2** (3) 269-81. A. Searle. (1972). *The Perception of Filmed Violence by High and Low Aggressive Adolescents,* unpublished Masters thesis, University of Leicester.

29. These are cited in detail below in Note 31.

30. A. Bandura, D. Ross, and S.A. Ross. (1963). 'Imitation of Film-Mediated Aggressive Models', *Journal of Abnormal and Social Psychology,* **66**, 3-11.

31. A. Bandura. (1962). 'Social Learning through Imitation', *Nebraska Symposium on Motivation, 1962,* Ed. M.R. Jones, University of Nebraska Press, Lincoln, Nebraska.
A. Bandura. (1965). 'Vicarious Processes: A Case of No-Trial Learning', in *Advances in Experimental Social Psychology, Volume II,* Ed. L. Berkowitz, Academic Press, New York.
A. Bandura, D. Ross and S.A. Ross. (1961). 'Transmission of Aggression Through Imitation of Aggressive Models', *Journal of Abnormal and Social Psychology*, **63**, 575-82.

A. Bandura, D. Ross, and S.A. Ross. (1963). 'Imitation of Film-Mediated Aggressive Models', *Journal of Abnormal and Social Psychology,* **66,** 3-11.

A. Bandura, D. Ross and S.A. Ross. (1963), 'Vicarious Reinforcement and Imitative Learning', *Journal of Abnormal and Social Psychology*, **67,** 601-7.

J. Bryan and T. Schwartz. (1971). 'Effects of Film Material upon Children's Behavior', *Psychological Bulletin,* **75,** 50-59.

D. Hicks. (1965). 'Imitation and Retention of Film-Mediated Aggressive Peer and Adult Models', *Journal of Personality and Social Psychology*, **2,** 97-100.

B.H. Kniveton and G.M. Stephenson. (1970). 'The Effect of Pre-Experience on Imitation of an Aggressive Film Model', *British Journal of Social and Clinical Psychology*, **9,** 31-36.

B.H. Kniveton and G.M. Stephenson. (1972). 'The Effects of Social Class on Imitation in a Pre-Experience Situation', *British Journal of Social and Clinical Psychology,* **11,** 225-34.

R. Liebert and R. Baron. (1971). *Effects of Symbolic Modeling on Children's Interpersonal Aggression,* unpublished manuscript. Read at the meeting of the Society for Research in Child Development.

R. Walters, M. Leat, and L. Mezei. (1963). 'Inhibition and Disinhibition of Responses Through Empathetic Learning', *Canadian Journal of Psychology,* **17,** 235-43.

32. A. Bandura. (1963). 'The Role of Imitation in Personality Development'. *The Journal of Nursery Education*, April pp.207-15.

33. R. Hartley. (1964). *A Review and Evaluation of Recent Studies on the Impact of Violence (Including Also Certain Related Papers)* CBS Inc., New York, pp.19-20.

34. J.D. Halloran. (1970). 'The Social Effects of Television', *The Effects of Television*, Ed. J.D. Halloran, Panther, London.

35. Personal communication.

36. D. Howitt. (1972). 'Effects of Aggressive Modeling Upon Nonimitative Aggression', *Catalogue of Selected Documents in Psychology*, **2,** 114-15. •

37. D. Howitt and G. Cumberbatch. (1971). *The Ethnology of Imitation,* unpublished manuscript, Centre for Mass Communication Research, University of Leicester.

38. M. Whitehouse. (1967). *Cleaning Up T.V.*, Blandford, London.

M. Whitehouse. (1971). *Who does She Think She is?,* New English Library, London.

39. R. Walters and D. Willows. (1968). 'Imitative Behavior of Disturbed and Nondisturbed Children Following Exposure to Aggressive and Nonaggressive Models', *Child Development*, **39,** 79-89.

40. Frederick Wertham is an exponent of this view.

41. K. Lorenz. (1966). *On Aggression,* Harcourt Brace Jovanovich, New York.
42. S.M. Berger. (1962). 'Conditioning Through Vicarious Instigation', *Psychological Review,* **69,** 450-66.
43. R.S. Lazarus and E. Alfert. (1964). 'Short Circuiting of Threat by Experimentally Altering Cognitive Appraisal', *Journal of Abnormal and Social Psychology,* **69,** 195-205.
    R. Lazarus, E. Opton, M. Nomikes, and N. Rukin. (1965). The Principle of Short-Circuiting of Threat: Further Evidence', *Journal of Personality,* **33,** 622-35.
44. V.B. Cline, R.G. Croft, and S. Courrier. (1972). *The Desensitization of Children to Television Violence,* unpublished Manuscript, University of Utah. This reports the emotional responses of high and low viewers of television violence differ — low viewers have most emotional response (even to non-violent segments).
45. J.L. Howard, C.B. Reifler, and M.B. Liptain. (1971). 'Effects of Exposure to Pornography', in *Technical Report of the Commission on Obscenity and Pornography, Volume VIII: Erotica and Social Behavior.* U.S. Government Printing Office, Washington, D.C., pp. 97-132.
    See also: J. Averill, E. Malmstrom, A. Koriat, and R. Lazarus. (1972). 'Habituation to Complex Emotional Stimuli', *Journal of Abnormal Psychology,* **80,** 20-8.
46. D. Howitt. (1972). 'Attitudes Towards Violence and Mass Media Exposure', *Gazette,* **18,** (4), 208-34.
47. W. Weiss. (1969). 'Effects of the Mass Media of Communication', in *The Handbook of Social Psychology, Volume 5,* Eds. G. Lindzey and E. Aronson, Addison-Wesley, Reading, Mass. pp.77-195.
48. G. Gerbner. (1971). 'Violence in Television Drama: Trends and Symbolic Functions', in *Television and Social Behavior, Volume 1: Content and Control,* Eds. G.A. Comstock and E.A. Rubinstein, U.S. Government Printing Office, Washington, D.C., pp.28-187.
49. D. Howitt. (1972). 'Attitudes Towards Violence and Mass Media Exposure', *Gazette,* **18** (4), 208-34.
50. G. Cumberbatch. (1971). *The Public Image.,* unpublished Manuscript, Centre for Mass Communication Research, University of Leicester.
51. S.H. Lovibond. (1967). 'The Effect of Media Stressing Crime and Violence upon Children's Attitudes', *Social Problems,* **15,** 91-100.
52. D. Howitt. (1972). 'Attitudes Towards Violence and Mass Media Exposure', *Gazette,* **18** (4), 208-34.
53. P. Hartmann and C. Husband. (1974). *Racism and the Mass Media,* Davis-Poynter, London.
54. D. Howitt. (1972). 'Attitudes Towards Violence and Mass Media

Exposure', *Gazette.* **18**, (4), 208-34.

55. G. Gerbner. (1969). 'The Television World of Violence', in *Mass Media and Violence*, Eds. R.K. Baker and S.J. Ball, U.S. Government Printing Office, Washington, D.C. pp.311-39.

56. J.R. Dominick and B.S. Greenberg. (1971). 'Attitudes Toward Violence: The Interaction of Television, Family Attitudes, and Social Class', in *Television and Social Behavior, Volume 3: Television and Adolescent Aggressiveness.* Eds. G.A. Comstock and E.A. Rubinstein, U.S. Government Printing Office, Washington, D.C. pp.314-35.

57. J. McLeod, C. Atkin and S. Chaffee. (1971). 'Adolescents, Parents and Television Use: Adolescent Self-Report Measures from Maryland and Wisconsin Samples', in *Television and Social Behavior, Volume 3: Television and Adolescent Aggressiveness,* Eds. G.A. Comstock and E.A. Rubinstein, U.S. Government Printing Office, Washington, D.C., pp.239-313.

58. B.S. Greenberg. (1973). *British Children and Televised Violence.* Report presented at the annual convention of the Association for Education in Journalism meeting at Colorado State University, August.

59. J. McLeod, C. Atkin and S. Chaffee. (1971). 'Adolescents, Parents and Television Use: Adolescent Self-Report Measures from Maryland and Wisconsin Samples', in *Television and Social Behavior, Volume 3, Television and Adolescent Aggressiveness,* Eds. G.A. Comstock and E.A. Rubinstein, U.S. Government Printing Office, Washington, D.C. pp.239-313.

60. K. Heinrich. (1960). *Filmerleben, Filmwirkung, Filmerziehung.* Hermann Schroedel, Berlin.

61. See earlier discussion of identification.

62. S. Feshbach and R. Singer. (1971). *Television and Aggression.* Jossey Bass, San Francisco.

63. W. Schramm, J. Lyle and E.B. Parker. (1961). *Television in the Lives of Our Children.* Stanford University Press.

64. E. Menzies. (1972). 'The Effects of Repeated Exposure to Televised Violence Upon Attitutdes Towards Violence Among Youthful Offenders', *FCI Research Reports,* **4** (5), 1-43.
    E. Menzies. (1971). 'Preferences in Television Content Among Violent Prisoners', *FCI Research Reports* **3**(1), 1-29.

65. See G. Cumberbatch and D. Howitt. (1974). *Social Communication and War: The Mass Media.* Paper read at Conference on Social Communication and War at the Universite Libre, Brussels and published in the proceedings of this conference.

66. L. Festinger. (1964). 'Behavioral Support for Opinion Change', *Public Opinion Quarterly,* **8**, 404-17.

67 H.L. Friedman and R.L. Johnson. (1971). 'Mass Media Use and

Aggression: A Pilot Study', in *Television and Social Behavior, Volume 3, Television and Adolescent Aggressiveness*, Eds. G.A. Comstock and E.A. Rubinstein, U.S. Government Printing Office, Washington, D.C., pp.336-60.

68. M.A. Hanratty, R.M. Liebert, L.W. Morris and L.E. Fernandez. (1969). 'Imitation of Film-Mediated Aggression Against Live and Inanimate Victims', *Proceedings of the 77th Annual Convention of the American Psychological Association*, 4, 457-58.

NOTES TO CHAPTER 5

1. J.D. Halloran, R.L. Brown and D.C. Chaney. (1970). *Television and Delinquency*, Leicester University Press, p.178.

2. The Surgeon General's Scientific Advisory Committee on Television and Social Behavior. (1972). *Television and Growing Up: The Impact of Televised Violence*, U.S. Government Printing Office, Washington, D.C. p.181.

3. The Surgeon General's Scientific Advisory Committee on Television and Social Behavior. (1972). *Television and Growing Up: The Impact of Televised Violence,* U.S. Government Printing Office, Washington, D.C. p.146.

4. There is, however, evidence to suggest that viewing and preferences are not the same thing at all. For example, middle-class individuals often claim to prefer 'cultural' programmes but their viewing patterns differ little from those of the working class. See A.S.C. Ehrenberg and G.J. Goodhardt (1969). 'Practical Applications of the Duplication of Viewing Law'. *Journal of the Market Research Society,* 11, 1, 6-24 for an account of this.

5. A recent survey of leisure in Great Britain showed that people devote more hours to television viewing than to any other leisure activity and devote more days to it than any activity other than newspaper reading. See *The Future of Broadcasting: Preliminary Report* (1973), unpublished manuscript. Centre for Mass Communication Research, University of Leicester.

6. M. Lefkowitz, L. Eron, L. Walder and L.R. Huesmann. (1971). 'Television Violence and Child Aggression: A Follow Up Study', in *Television and Social Behaviour, Volume 3: Television and Adolescent Aggressiveness,* Eds. G.A. Comstock and E.A. Rubinstein, U.S. Government Printing Office, Washington, D.C. pp.35-135.
This is a longitudinal development of an earlier study: L. Eron. (1963). 'Relationship of TV Viewing Habits and Aggressive Behavior in Children', *Journal of Abnormal and Social Psychology,* 67, 193-96. The same authors have published an abbreviated version of the major report: L.D. Eron, L.R. Huesmann, M.M. Lefkowitz, and L.O. Walder. (1972). 'Does Television Violence

Cause Aggression?' *American Psychologist,* **27**, 253-63.

This last report received considerable adverse criticism in the pages of the *American Psychologist* from the following:

G. Becker. (1972). 'Causal Analysis in R-R Studies: Television Violence and Aggression', *American Psychologist,* **27**, 967-68.

D. Howitt. (1972). 'Television and Aggression: A Counterargument', *American Psychologist,* **27**, 969-70.

R.M. Kaplan. (1972). 'On Television as a Cause of Aggression', *American Psychologist,* **27**, 968-69

H. Kay. (1972). 'Weaknesses in the Television-Causes-Aggression Analysis' by Eron *et al. American Psychologist,* **27**, 970-73.

The authors had opportunity to dismiss these criticisms in the following:

L.R. Huesmann, L.D. Eron, M.M. Lefkowitz and L.O. Walder. (1973). 'Television Violence and Aggression: The Causal Effect Remains', *American Psychologist,* **28**, 617-20.

It is a tribute either to the profound adequacy or the profound inadequacy of the content of this chapter that the authors did not deal with Howitt's argument which forms the basis of this entire chapter!

7. H. Kay. (1972) 'Weaknesses in the Television-Causes-Aggression Analysis by Eron *et al.' American Psychologist,* **27**, 970-73.

8. J.R. Milavsky and B. Pekowsky. (1973). *Exposure to TV 'Violence' and Aggressive Behaviour in Boys, Examined as Process: A Status Report of a Longitudinal Study,* unpublished manuscript, Department of Social Research, National Broadcasting Company.

9. J. McLeod, C. Atkin and S. Chaffee. (1971). 'Adolescents, Parents, and Television Use: Self-Report and Other Report Measures from the Wisconsin Sample', in *Television and Social Behavior, Volume 3, Television and Adolescent Aggressiveness,* Eds. G.A. Comstock and E.A. Rubinstein U.S. Government Printing Office, Washington, D.C. pp. 239-313.

There are other related studies by these authors reported in this volume but since they deal exclusively with the area of attitudes rather than acts they are of no concern in this chapter.

10. E. Karp. (1954). *Crime Comic Book Role Preferences,* unpublished Doctoral Dissertation, New York University.

11. J.D. Halloran, R.L. Brown and D.C. Chaney. (1970). *Television and Delinquency,* Leicester University Press.

12. H.T. Bassett, J.E. Cowden and M.F. Cohen. (1968). 'The Audio-Visual Viewing Habits of a Selected Subgroup of Delinquents', *Journal of Genetic Psychology,* **112**, 37-41.

J.E. Cowden, H.T. Bassett, and M.F. Cohen. (1969). 'An Analysis of Some Correlations Between Fantasy-Aggression and Aggressive

Behavior Among Institutionalized Delinquents', *Journal of Genetics, Psychology,* **114,** 179-83. In this study assaultive incarcerated adolescents were compared with non-assaultive incarcerated adolescents.

13. E. Pfuhl. (1960). *The Relationship of Mass Media to Reported Delinquent Behavior,* unpublished Doctoral Dissertation, Washington State University. Ann Arbor, Michigan: University Microfilms. No. 61-1308.

    E. Pfuhl. (1970). 'Mass Media and Reported Delinquent Behavior: A Negative Case', in *The Sociology of Crime and Delinquency,* Eds. M. Wolfgang, L. Savity and N. Johnston, Wiley, New York.

14. See J.D. Halloran, R.L. Brown, and D.C. Chaney. (1970). *Television and Delinquency,* Leicester University Press, pp. 73-80 for detailed criticism.

    Pfuhl took objection to Howitt's treatment of his data in the following: E. Pfuhl. (1973). 'Rebuttal to Howitt', *American Psychologist,* **28,** 533-34.

    Howitt replied in:

    D. Howitt. (1973). *Rebuttal to Howitt: The Reply,* unpublished manuscript, Centre for Mass Communication Research, University of Leicester

    Howitt's rejection of Pfuhl's interpretation of how his own data is based largely on the fact that Pfuhl uses a purely statistical argument to reject the relationship between media violence and delinquency. Howitt argues that Pfuhl's data do not follow a random pattern as would be implied by his conclusions but that there is a systematic relationship between exposure to certain media and delinquency which is difficult to explain on the basis of chance.

15. J. McIntyre and J. Teevan. (1971). 'Television and Deviant Behavior', in *Television and Social Behavior, Volume 3: Television and Adolescent Aggressiveness,* Eds. G.A. Comstock and E.A. Rubinstein, U.S. Government Printing Office, Washington, D.C. pp. 383-434.

16. See S. Box. (1971). *Deviance, Reality and Society,* Hall, Rinehart and Winston, London.

17. D.C. Clark and W.B. Blankenburg. (1971). 'Trends in Violent Content in Selected Mass Media', in *Television and Social Behavior, Volume 1: Content and Control,* Eds. G.A. Comstock and E.A. Rubinstein, U.S. Government Printing Office, Washington, D.C.

18. H.T. Himmelweit, A.N. Oppenheim, and P. Vince. (1958). *Television and the Child,* Oxford University Press, London.

    'In our survey we found no more aggressive, maladjusted, or delinquent behaviour among viewers than among controls. Seeing violence on television is not likely to turn well-adjusted children into aggressive delinquents; there must be a predisposition for them to be affected in this way. Nor do children as a whole translate television experience into action. It may happen in extreme cases where children have a strong desire to be aggressive or to perform a delinquent act, and for whom constant watching of programmes with an explosive content may be the last straw.' p. 215.

19. E. Menzies. (1971). 'Preferences in Television Content Among Violent Prisoners', *FCI Research Report* **(1)**, 1-29.
20. D.B. Mills. (1971). *An Exploration of the Relationship Between Television Habits, Preferences, and Aggression in Sixth-Grade Boys*, unpublished Diploma of Education Thesis, University of Maryland. Ann Arbor, Michigan, University Microfilms, 72-10080.
21. E. Pfuhl. (1960). *The Relationship of Mass Media to Reported Delinquent Behavior*, unpublished Doctoral Dissertation, Washington State University, Ann Arbor, Michigan: University Microfilms No. 61-1308.
    E. Pfuhl. (1970). 'Mass Media and Reported Delinquent Behavior: A Negative Case', in *The Sociology of Crime and Delinquency.* Eds. M. Wolfgang, L. Savitz, and N. Johnston, Wiley, New York.
22. F. Shuttleworth and M. May. (1933). *The Social Conduct and Attitudes of Movie Fans*, Macmillan, New York.
23. P.G. Cressey and F.M. Thrasher. (1933). *Boys, Movies and City Streets,* Macmillan, New York.
24. W. Healy and A. Bronner. (1936). *New Light on Delinquency and Its Treatment*, Yale University Press, New Haven.
25. E. Karp. (1954). *Crime Comic Book Role Preferences*, unpublished Doctoral Dissertations, New York University.
26. E. Pfuhl. (1960). *The Relationship of Mass Media to Reported Delinquent Behavior*, unpublished Doctoral Dissertation, Washington State University, Ann Arbor, Michigan: University Microfilms 61-1308.
    E. Pfuhl. (1970). 'Mass Media and Reported Delinquent Behavior: A Negative Case', in *The Sociology of Crime and Delinquency*, Eds. M. Wolfgang, L. Savitz and N. Johnston, Wiley, New York.
27. See Note 26.
28. E.A. Ricuitti. (1951). 'Children and Radio', *Genetic Psychology Monographs*, **64**, 69-143.
29. Transistors alone did not bring about this change. There is reason to believe that television brought about reformulations of the role of radio.
30. We are thinking of the anti-comic movement of the 1950s here.
31. T.B. Hoult. (1949). 'Comic Books and Juvenile Delinquency', *Sociology and Social Research*, **33**, 279-84.
32. See Note 31 above. However one must note that the nature of the content of comic books has changed in this period due to the

anti-comic wars of the fifties.

33. See Note 31 above.
34. H.S. Lewin. (1953). 'Facts and Fears About the Comics', *The Nation's Schools*, Vol III, pp.46-8. Quoted in E. Pfuhl. (1960). *The Relationship of Mass Media to Reported Delinquent Behavior*, unpublished Doctoral Dissertation, Washington State University, Ann Arbor, Michigan: University Microfilms 61-1308.
35. See Note 34.
36. See Note 34.
37. See Note 34.
38. Quoted in H.J. Forman. (1935). *Our Movie Made Children*, Macmillan, New York. The quotation is from a chapter of a book in preparation when Whitley died. The work was to have been part of the Payne Fund Studies.
    Other media have been shown to serve functions other than that directly implied by their content.
39. B. Berelson. (1948). 'What Missing the Newspapers Means', in *The Process and Effects of Mass Communication*, Ed. W. Schramm, University of Illinois Press. 1954.
40. I.L. Friedman and R.L. Johnson. (1971). 'Mass Media Use and Aggression: A Pilot Study', in *Television and Social Behavior Volume 3. Television and Adolescent Aggressiveness*. Eds. G.A. Comstock and E.A. Rubinstein, U.S. Government Printing Office, Washington, D.C. pp.336-60.
41. W.L. Rivers, T. Peterson and J.W. Jensen. (1971). *The Mass Media and Modern Society*, Rinehart, San Francisco.
42. D. Howitt. (1972). 'Television and Aggression: A Counterargument', *American Psychologist*, **27**, 969-70.
43. R. Dembo. (1972). *Aggression and Media Use Among English Working-Class Youths*, unpublished Report, Centre for Mass Communication Research, University of Leicester.
    R. Dembo. (1972). 'Life Style and Media Use Among English Working-Class Youths,*Gazette: International Journal for Mass Communication Studies*, **18**, 212-29.
    R. Dembo. (1973). 'Critical Factors in Understanding Adolescent Aggression',*Social Psychiatry*, **8**, 212-19.
    R. Dembo. (1974). 'Gratifications Found in Media by British Teenage Boys', *Journalism Quarterly*, in Press.
    R. Dembo and R. McCron. (1975). 'Social Mapping and Media Use', in *Children and Television*, Ed. J.R. Brown, Cassell and Collier Macmillan, London.
44. R. Brown and M. O'Leary. (1971). 'Pop music in an English Secondary School System', *American Behavioral Scientist*, **14**,(3), 401-13.
45. For a more technical account of these ideas see: D. Howitt and R.

Dembo. (1974). 'A Subcultural Account of Media Effects', *Human Relations*, **27**, 25-42.

NOTES TO CHAPTER 6

,1. S.H. Frailberg. (1969). 'The Mass Media: New Schoolhouse for Children', in *Violence in the Streets*, Ed. S. Endleman, Duckworth, London. pp.119-34.
2. See J. McLeod and G. O'Keefe. (1972). 'The Socialization Perspective and Communicative Behavior', in *Current Perspectives in Mass Communication Research*, Eds. F.G. Kline and P.J. Tichenor, Sage, Beverly Hills.
   S.H. Chaffee. (1972). 'The Interpersonal Context of Mass Communication', in *Current Perspectives in Mass Communication Research,* Eds. F.G. Kline and P.J. Tichenor, Sage, Beverly Hills. pp.95-120.
3. G.W. de Rath. (1963). *The Effects of Verbal Instructions on Imitative Aggression*, unpublished Ph.D. thesis, Michigan State University.
4. S.H. Chaffee and H.M. McLeod. (1971). 'Adolescent Television Use in the Family Context', in *Television and Social Behavior. Volume III: Television and Adolescent Aggressiveness*, Eds. G.A. Comstock and E.A. Rubinstein, U.S. Government Printing Office, Washington, D.C. pp.142-79.
   J.M. McLeod, C.K. Atkin and S.H. Chaffee. (1971). 'Adolescents, Parents, and Television Use: Adolescent Self-Report Measures from Maryland and Wisconsin Samples', in *Television and Social Behavior. Volume III: Television and Adolescent Aggressiveness*, Eds. G.A. Comstock and E.A. Rubinstein, U.S. Government Printing Office, Washington, D.C. pp.173-238.
   J.M. McLeod, C.K. Atkin, and S.H. Chaffee. (1971). See above, pp.239-313.
5. J.M. McLeod, C.K. Atkin, and S.H. Chaffee. (1971). See above, pp.373-74.
6. J. McIntyre and J. Teevan. (1971). 'Television Violence and Deviant Behavior', in *Television and Social Behavior. Volume 3. Television and Adolescent Aggressiveness* Eds. G.A. Comstock and E.A. Rubinstein, U.S. Government Printing Office, Washington, D.C. pp.383-435.
7. See above.
8. J. Lyle and H.R. Hoffman. (1971). 'Children's Use of Television and Other Media', in *Television and Social Behavior. Volume 4: Television in Day-to-Day Life: Patterns of Use*, Eds. E.A. Rubinstein, G.A. Comstock, and J.P. Murray, U.S. Government Printing Office, Washington, D.C. pp.129-256.

9. G. Phelps and E. Eyre-Brook. (1973). *A Study of Children's Reactions to the Film 'The Fourteen'*, unpublished manuscript, Centre for Mass Communication Research, University of Leicester.

10. D. Howitt. (1972). *Trash — Some Audience Reactions*, unpublished manuscript, Centre for Mass Communication Research, University of Leicester.

11. In an ongoing study of pre-school children by the senior author, it has been noted that heavily researched programmes such as *Sesame Street* may invoke distress reactions in certain children.

12. H.T. Himmelweit, A.N. Oppenheim, and P. Vince. (1958). *Television and the Child*, Oxford University Press, London.

13. British Broadcasting Corporation. (1962).'Violence in Television Programmes', *Television Quarterly,* 1, 61.

14. D.C. Clarke and W.B. Blankenburg. (1971). 'Trends in Violent Content in Selected Mass Media', in *Television and Social Behavior. Volume 1: Content and Control,* Eds. G.A. Comstock and E.A. Rubinstein, U.S. Government Printing Office, Washington, D.C. pp.188-243.

15. Clarke and Blankenburg. p.235.

16. T.F. Baldwin and C. Lewis. (1971). 'Violence in Television: The Industry Looks at Itself', in *Television and Social Behavior, Volume 1: Content and Control*, Eds. G.A. Comstock and E.A. Rubinstein, U.S. Government Printing Office, Washington D.C. pp.290-373.

17 Baldwin and Lewis pp.314-35

18. Baldwin and Lewis pp.314.

19. Baldwin and Lewis pp.328 and 340.

20. J.D. Halloran. (1970). *The Effects of Television*, Panther, London.

21. J.D. Halloran and P. Croll. (1971). 'Television Programs in Great Britain', in *Television and Social Behavior. Volume 1: Content and Control*, Eds. G.A. Comstock and E.A. Rubinstein, U.S. Government Printing Office, Washington D.C., pp.415-92.

22. D. Howitt and G. Cumberbatch. (1974). 'Audience Perceptions of Violent Television Content',*Communication Research,* 1, (2), 204-223

23. British Broadcasting Corporation. (1972). *Violence on Television: Programme Content and Viewer Perceptions*.

24. B.S. Greenberg and T.F. Gordon. (1971). 'Children's Perceptions of Television Violence: A Replication', in *Television and Social Behavior. Volume 5: Television Effects: Further Explorations* Eds. G.A. Comstock, E.A. Rubinstein and J.P. Murray, U.S. Government Printing Office, Washington, D.C. pp.211-30.
   B.S. Greenberg and T.F. Gordon. (1971). 'Perceptions of Violence in Television Programs: Critics and the Public', in *Television and Social Behavior. Volume 1: Content and Control*. Eds. G.A. Comstock and E.A. Rubinstein, U.S. Government Printing Office,

Washington, D.C. pp.244-56.

B.S. Greenberg and T.F. Gordon. (1971). 'Social Class and Racial Differences in Children's Perceptions of Televised Violence', in *Television and Social Behavior. Volume 5: Television's Effects: Further Explorations*, Eds. G.A. Comstock, E.A. Rubinstein, and J.P. Murray, U.S. Government Printing Office, Washington, D.C. pp.185-210.

25. A. Searle. (1972). *The Perception of Filmed Violence by High and Low Aggressive Adolescents*, unpublished Masters thesis, University of Leicester.

26. British Broadcasting Corporation. (1972). *Violence on Television: Programme Content and Viewer Perceptions*.

27. S. Feshbach. (1971). 'Reality and Fantasy in Filmed Violence', in *Television and Social Behavior. Volume 2: Television and Social Learning*, Eds. J.P. Murray, E.A. Rubinstein, and G.A. Comstock, U.S. Government Printing Office, Washington D.C.

    L. Berkowitz and J. Alioto. (1973). 'The Meaning of an Observed Event as a Determinant of Its Aggressive Consequences', *Journal of Personality and Social Psychology*, 28 (2), 206-17.

28. D.C. Clark and W.B. Blankenburg. (1971). 'Trends in Violent Content in Selected Mass Media', in *Television and Social Behavior. Volume 1: Content and Controls*, Eds. G.A. Comstock and E.A. Rubinstein, U.S. Government Printing Office, Washington, D.C. pp.188-243

29 For further discussion see P. Elliott. (1972). *The Making of a Television Series*, Constable, London.

30. G. Cumberbatch and D. Howitt. (1974). 'Identification with Aggressive Television Characters', in *Determinants and Origins of Aggressive Behavior*, Eds. W.W. Hartup and J. Dewit, Mouton, The Hague.

31. J.D. Halloran and M. Gurevitch. (1971). *Broadcaster/Researcher Co-operation in Mass Communication Research*, Centre for Mass Communication Research, University of Leicester.

AUTHOR INDEX

161

SUBJECT INDEX